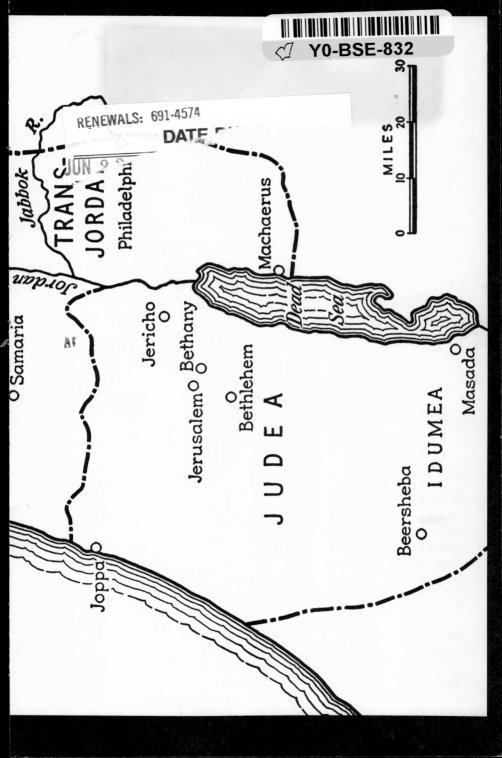

R.

Jabbok

TRANS-
JORDAN

Philadelphia

Jordan

Machaerus

Dead   *Sea*

Samaria

Jericho

Bethany

Jerusalem

Bethlehem

J U D E A

Masada

Beersheba

I D U M E A

Joppa

MILES

30

20

10

0

A Life of Jesus

A Life of Jesus

by

EDGAR J. GOODSPEED

GREENWOOD PRESS, PUBLISHERS
WESTPORT, CONNECTICUT

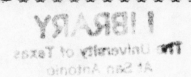

Library of Congress Cataloging in Publication Data

Goodspeed, Edgar Johnson, 1871-1962.
   A life of Jesus.

   Reprint of the ed. published by Harper, New York.
   Includes bibliographical references and index.
   1. Jesus Christ--Biography. 2. Christian
biography--Palestine.   I.   Title.
BT301.G73   1979   232.9'01 [B]   78-21540
ISBN 0-313-20728-3

Reprinted with the permission of Harper & Row, Publishers, Inc.

Reprinted in 1979 by Greenwood Press, Inc.
51 Riverside Avenue, Westport, CT 06880

Printed in the United States of America

10 9 8 7 6 5 4 3 2 1

In ever loving memory of
ELFLEDA
1880–1949
who asked me to write this book

CONTENTS

7

8 *Contents*

ACKNOWLEDGMENTS

Acknowledgment is gratefully made to the University of Chicago Press for permission to make free use of the text of *The New Testament: An American Translation,* in this biography; and to The Macmillan Company, New York, for permission to use three or four striking sentences from *Religion in the Making,* by Professor Alfred North Whitehead (copyright, 1926, by The Macmillan Company). Professor Eric L. Titus, Ph.D., of the University of Southern California, has very kindly read the book in manuscript and offered many helpful suggestions, though he is not to be held responsible for the views expressed in it. President Ernest C. Colwell, of the University of Chicago, has on some points given me his encouragement.

Preface

"The life of Jesus Christ cannot be written." This has long been a commonplace with historians and biographers.

And yet what life has been so often written? Not, indeed, with the precision and fullness of information the ideal biography demands, and yet more movingly and tellingly than any other person's history. For the story of Jesus and how he flashed like a meteor across the sky of his generation and this world cannot be told too often. Adequately it can indeed never be written, but though all other life stories fade from the memory of men, it must never be forgotten, for its sheer influence on human thought, human relations and human destiny, and for its incomparable contribution to man's faith in good and goodness. But who is sufficient for these things?

No biography of Jesus can be written without emotion. To try to do so is to miss what is basic and central in it all. For it is a record of great emotions—of commission, temptation, devotion, compassion, surrender and sacrifice. If one is a stranger to these emotions, he can never penetrate to the meaning of Jesus' life and ministry, for he was a man of great emotions.

But of course they were more than emotions; they were convictions. And anyone who is a stranger to convictions cannot hope to read the riddle of the personality of Jesus, the most baffling and the most important in history.

It is a sobering and yet a thrilling experience even to try to write a sketch of the ministry of Jesus. It is of course the most tremendous drama in human history, and the most paradoxical. Its apparent failure was its stupendous success.

Introduction

The earthly life of Jesus has come down to us in the records of the four gospels of Matthew, Mark, Luke and John, with some secondary echoes in a score or more of later, uncanonical gospels, of most of which only fragments now exist. These last are, however, so obviously based on the first four that they present no substantial addition to them except a striking saying or two, which may possibly be authentic.

Of the original four, John is the latest, and the most obviously Greek in origin, being an admirable effort to present the great religious values of the new faith in terms immediately intelligible to the Greek mind. Its emphasis is upon the Christian's religious experience of Jesus as a spiritual force. It is therefore of immense importance as evidence of his spiritual influence, rather than of the course of events during his life on earth. Its doctrines are strongly influenced by the collected letters of Paul, and it was written probably in the circle of Ephesus early in the second century after Christ. Very soon after its publication, the gospels were collected by Christian enterprise, and published, notwithstanding their differences, as a collection, forming, we may fairly say, the most successful piece of publishing in all history, since no other publishing enterprise has ever equaled them in circulation or influence. We may say of them that while the fourth gospel in the series winningly presents the Christ of experience, the first three embody so much primitive Christian tradition that they bring us close to the Jesus of history, in the few portentous months of his earthly ministry.

The earliest of the three was the Gospel of Mark, probably written by the cousin of Barnabas of that name who accompanied Paul and Barnabas on the first part of the first missionary journey and was with Paul long afterward at Rome when he wrote his letter to the Colossians. From an early tradition, preserved by Papias of Hierapolis, about A.D. 140, we gather that when Peter afterward came to Rome to preach, his Aramaic sermons were translated sentence by sentence into Greek for his Greek hearers in the church of Rome (which was a Greek-speaking church until the middle of the third century) by translators or interpreters familiar with both languages, one of whom was Mark, and that Mark, after Peter's sudden, terrible martyrdom, gathered from his recollections of what he had heard Peter say the parts relating to the life and teaching of Jesus, and so produced the Gospel of Mark. Many things in the book seem to confirm this account of its origin, so that we may be sure it brings us closer to the scenes and action of Jesus' ministry than the later Gospels of Matthew and of Luke, which are manifestly based upon it. We observe that what we may call the intimate narrative begins with the call of Simon, that is, Peter; that the action continues in Peter's house, and in his boat; in a number of scenes only Peter, James and John are present; at Caesarea Philippi it is Peter who speaks up to answer Jesus' question, and who rebukes Jesus, and is rebuked; and of his three denials at the trial only Peter could have known and told.

I Peter, written probably about A.D. 95, speaks in behalf of "your sister church in Babylon and Mark my son." Babylon is the regular apocalyptic name for Rome, in the Revelation, Baruch, the Letter of Jeremiah and II Esdras, in the Apocrypha. Mark was not Peter's son, except in the figurative, spiritual sense, and the coupling of Mark, Peter and Rome together can hardly point to anything less than the recording of Peter's testimony, by Mark, in Rome. I Peter 5:13 is in effect an allusion to what we know as the Gospel of Mark, as embodying the reminiscences of Peter and as emanating from the church at Rome. When it is remembered that I Peter was written to save the churches of Asia Minor from the vengeful attitude toward their persecutors which the Revelation of John seemed to inculcate (18:6, 20; compare I Peter 2:13-17; 3:8, 9), it will be seen that the church at Rome needed all the authority it could muster to offset the exalted claims of direct inspiration made in the Revelation of John.

Thus the incidental external evidence as to the origin of Mark (except for the probable presence of a "little apocalypse" in Chapter 13) agrees very well with the internal evidence which the book itself gives as to its probable origin.

The Gospel of Mark presents Jesus as a Doer, a Man

of Action. But the Gospel of Matthew shows him as pre-
eminently the Teacher, setting forth his message in six great
sermons, beginning with the Sermon on the Mount. The
Gospels of Matthew and of Luke both have much to tell
us, especially of the further teachings of Jesus, not included in the rather factual narrative of Mark. The vivid
and convincing account of the Temptation we owe to them.
Matthew was written some ten years after Mark, about
A.D. 80, and Luke, as the first volume of Luke's two-
volume history, Luke-Acts, about A.D. 90. The further advance of Christian thought and life is naturally reflected
in some degree in them, and read back into the times and
teachings of Jesus.

But before the gospels were written, there was an unwritten oral gospel, or at least a story of Jesus' life and
teaching, which people who came into the Christian movement and joined the church would learn by heart. It was
probably never written down, nor has any part of it ever
been definitely recognized in our written gospels, but its
influence occasionally gleams through Paul's letters, for it
was the only gospel known to him. As Paul's letters were
written between A.D. 50 and 61, they antedate the earliest
of our written gospels, the Gospel of Mark, by from ten
to twenty years, being written between twenty and thirty
years after the death of Christ, so that the few words they
contain about the earthly life of Jesus are extraordinarily
early, and sometimes give us evidence of much importance.
We can gather echoes of this oral gospel from such sources
as Acts 20:35, I Clement to the Corinthians 13:1 and

46:7, Polycarp's Letter to the Philippians 2:3. Things taken from it are usually introduced with the words "Remember the words of the Lord Jesus," or "remembering what the Lord said in his teaching."

It was in this incipient form that the gospel story was known to Paul and quoted in I Corinthians 11:24, 25, verses which give us our oldest account of the Last Supper, and 15:5, 6, so important as the earliest account of the Resurrection.

The writings of Paul and the evangelists were only the beginning of a great writing movement on the part of the early Christians, and these writings were widely circulated and read among the churches, so that there was much interpretation of Jesus' teaching and of his life and death, and development of these interpretations in the books that followed, in the New Testament, the so-called Apostolic Fathers, the writings of the Christian defenders of the new religion, the apologists, and the resisters of schismatic and sectarian movements, such as that of Marcion about A.D. 140.

The death of Jesus, which at first seemed so bitterly to disappoint all the high Messianic hopes of his followers of a redeemed nation, which should lead the world into the kingdom of God, in the light of what he had said at the Last Supper, and of their new experience of his continued presence, took on a new and grander meaning. It was a great sacrifice, the Son of God offering himself up for the sins of mankind. This idea was suggested by Jesus' words at the Supper, when he spoke of his body as taking their place, and of his blood as ratifying the new covenant or agreement, as every ancient agreement of importance was ratified by the blood of some animal sacrifice. This appears in the very earliest account of the Supper that has come down to us, from the hand of Paul, in I Corinthians, Chapter 11, written only twenty-four years after Jesus' death, long before the writing of the earliest gospel.

The cross, which had at first been a symbol only of disgrace and utter defeat—crucifixion was the punishment of slaves and criminals—was thus transformed in a few short years into the symbol of sublime sacrifice and of redemption for all mankind. This has already happened even when Paul writes his letters, beginning in A.D. 50, some twenty years after Jesus' death.

We might reasonably hope for some light on Jesus from contemporary Jewish sources, but these are strangely disappointing. The aversion of first-century Palestinian Judaism to writing, its reliance on oral transmission alone for what it deemed important, the consequent loss or modification of much that was for a time preserved in this way and the committing of the rest to writing on in the second century, culminating in its written codification as the Mishnah toward A.D. 200 make the Jewish material dubious in date and vague in content. It has little that is definite to contribute. What would our position in church history be if we had nothing definite in the way of written books, until near the year 200—when Victor, as bishop of Rome, was taking it upon himself to excommunicate the Asian bishops for not agreeing with him on the date of Easter?

Tremendous developments had already taken place. But fortunately such is the wealth of early Christian literature during the preceding century and a half that we can trace their progress. For this we cannot be too grateful. This literature was wholly Greek, for it was only where the Christian movement entered the Greek world, of books and writers, that it began to express itself in writing (A.D. 50), in letters and then in books. Meantime, Aramaic-speaking Judaism with its avowed aversion to religious writing and its dependence on oral tradition went on its nonliterary way for a hundred and fifty years.

Yet we can even from what survives in the Mishnah recover something of the rabbinical background—the views of Shammai and Hillel—against which Jesus' teaching is silhouetted.

Josephus, the Jewish historian, who wrote his *Antiquities of the Jews* in Rome under Domitian, A.D. 81-96, finishing it in A.D. 93, speaks of Jesus twice, once casually, in *Antiquities* xx.9. 1, in connection with the stoning of James "the brother of Jesus who was called Christ" at the instigation of the high priest Ananus (Annas). The longer passage, which is found in *Antiquities* xviii.3. 3, reads thus:

"There arose at this time Jesus a wise man, if it is right to call him a man. For he was a doer of extraordinary acts, a teacher of men who are glad to receive the truth, and he drew to himself many Jews and many of the Greek race. He was the Christ. And when Pilate at the instance of the foremost men among us had sentenced him to be crucified, those who had first loved him did not cease to do so, for on the third day he appeared to them again, alive, since the divine prophets had foretold this and ten thousand other marvels about him. And even now the tribe of Christians named after him is not extinct."

This account of Jesus has seemed to many scholars too definitely Christian to have been written by a Jewish writer like Josephus (for if he wrote it he would seem to have been a Christian himself, which he was not), and so it has been variously disposed of, as an interpolation, or as in part interpolated. And yet there were certainly people called Christians in Rome as early as A.D. 64, as Tacitus shows, and they must have got their name from a leader called Christ, as Suetonius and Pliny soon showed by their accounts, and so a mention of Jesus substantially equivalent to this one, except perhaps for designating him as the Christ, may well have stood in Josephus' book, written in Rome in A.D. 81 to 93. We may reasonably believe so until some more ancient manuscript testimony appears to correct us.

In simple fact Jesus had already become the Christ of history, whatever Josephus thought of the Messiah of Jewish prophecy; Pliny, Suetonius and Tacitus all treat that as his name. But some touches in the paragraph—his possibly divine nature, his resurrection and countless marvels about him and his being the Christ—may be the additions of pious medieval scribes.

Nor must we lose sight of the few allusions to Jesus in the Greek and Latin historians of the first and second centuries. To some their evidence is disappointing, it is so small and casual. But it must be remembered that they wrote for the Roman world, a world so far removed from the kingdom of heaven which Jesus sought to inaugurate that it is a wonder they ever even mentioned him at all. It is hard for us moderns, in America at least, to envisage that Roman world, so brutal, callous, cruel, coarse. It was a world of slavery; if the slaves in it did not outnumber the free people, they came very near it. When Corinth was captured by Lucius Mummius in 146 B.C., the whole population was sold into slavery. Many of these slaves were better-educated people than their masters. The Romans thought nothing of crucifying people by the thousand. They found entertainment in seeing men and wild animals fight each other to death. Augustus in his *Res Gestae*, his "Achievements" composed for his epitaph by himself, as many scholars believe, reported that ten thousand men had fought in gladiatorial shows given the Roman public by him. He was proud of it. Unwanted babies were thrown out to die; kindhearted persons who picked them up and reared them could have them, or sell them, as slaves. In the latter part of the first century the most popular humorist at Rome was a man whose epigrams are many of them so obscene that modern publishers will not print them in translation. To such a world Jesus would not appeal, and it is easy to see why not. Christianity's early progress was not in that world at all, but in the Greek world, which was on a higher plane of sensibility and understanding.

And yet some Roman writers did mention Jesus, briefly of course. Tacitus in his *Annals* xv, 44, written probably between A.D. 110 and 120, explains how Nero, to escape the blame for the burning of Rome in A.D. 64, tried to throw it on the Christians:

Hence, to suppress the rumor, he falsely charged with the guilt, and punished with the most exquisite tortures, the persons commonly called Christians, who were hated for their enormities. Christus, the founder of that name, was put to death as a criminal, by Pontius Pilate, procurator of Judea, in the reign of Tiberius, but the pernicious superstition, repressed for a time, broke out again, not only through Judea, where the mischief originated, but through the city of Rome also, whither all things horrible and disgraceful flow from all quarters, as to a common receptacle, and where they are encouraged. Accordingly, first those were seized who confessed they were Christians; next, on their information, a vast multitude were convicted, not so much on the charge of burning the city, as of hating the human race. And in their deaths they were also made the subjects of sport, for they were covered with the hides of wild beasts, and worried to death by dogs, or nailed to crosses, or set fire to, and when day declined, burned to serve for nocturnal lights. Nero offered his own gardens for that spectacle. . . .

This was in August, A.D. 64.

The point in the *Annals* where Jesus might have been expected to be mentioned would have been in the chapters following Chapter 5 in book V, where the chapters which covered the years 29 and 30—just the period of Jesus' activity—are missing from the only manuscript of the first part of the *Annals*. But Tacitus could hardly have said more on such a subject than he does in the above quotation from xv, 44.

Suetonius, a gossipy individual, once Hadrian's private secretary, wrote his books between A.D. 98 and 138. In his *Lives of the Caesars,* "Claudius," Chapter 25, he says, "He [Claudius] banished from Rome all the Jews, who were continually making disturbances at the instigation of one Chrestus."

This is believed to be an allusion to Christ (Christus), his name being confused with the more familiar Greek and Latin name of Chrestus. From the way Christians talked of Christ's presence with them, pagans would naturally suppose Christ was living among them and causing all this excitement. Claudius' expulsion of the Jews from Rome (though Dio says he only forbade their meetings) is mentioned in Acts 18:2 as having caused Aquila and his wife Priscilla to leave Rome and move to Corinth.

Pliny the Younger in his letter to Trajan, written while Pliny was governor of Bithynia, in A.D. 112, raises the question about the Christians there, whom it seems to have been his duty to prosecute for following a non-authorized, or unlicensed, religion. Pliny inquires whether it is the "name" or the crimes attaching to the name that are to be punished. He writes the emperor that the Christians seem to be inoffensive people who gather before daybreak and sing a hymn to Christ as God, and swear not to commit crimes or wrongs. They then disperse and reassemble to eat a harmless meal together. Pliny evidently dislikes to take the extreme measures against these people that the law demands. But the temples had come to be deserted and the sacrifices stopped, and he had felt obliged to act. His letter is of about the date of the Gospel of John, which was written probably in the circle of Ephesus about A.D. 110.

Josephus wrote in Greek, in that Roman effort to revive Greek literature which the Flavian emperors promoted and financed. Pliny, Tacitus and Suetonius wrote in Latin.

A Life of Jesus

The life of Christ . . . has the decisiveness of a supreme ideal, and that is why the history of the world divides at this point of time.

ALFRED NORTH WHITEHEAD

CHAPTER I

Jesus' Childhood and Youth

Our first information about the lineage of Jesus is from the apostle Paul, in the opening lines of Romans, written only twenty-four or -five years after Jesus' death, where Paul speaks of him as descended from David. Of course there is not the slightest reason to doubt that he was so descended. With this statement the early gospels agree. Matthew and Luke are very explicit about it, and even Mark represents Jesus as accepting without objection and as a matter of course the salutation of Son of David, although Mark, and Matthew and Luke after him, describes Jesus as rather discounting his Davidic descent, when he said in the temple, with Psalm 110 in mind, "If David calls him lord, how can he be his son?"

But a thousand years had passed since David's prime—he reigned probably from 1013 to 973 B.C.—and almost if not quite every Jew in Palestine was probably descended from him by some line or other. Certainly it is a caricature of historical research to question an overwhelming probability, upon which the four gospels and the apostle Paul substantially agree.

Neither Paul nor Mark has occasion to speak of his

birthplace, but Matthew and Luke, while they have quite different accounts of his birth, and Luke in writing his gospel shows no acquaintance with the Gospel of Matthew, agree in placing Jesus' birth at David's home town of Bethlehem, a few miles south of Jerusalem. Some scholars deny that Jesus was born in Bethlehem, chiefly because there was in the prophets, as Matthew points out, 2:6, a prediction that the Messiah would arise from there (Micah 5:2). But the evangelist Matthew also found an oracle that seemed to connect Jesus with Nazareth (2:23) and this has led some scholars to doubt that he even lived there. It is evident that such methods of research simply defeat themselves. Jesus himself, moreover, never made anything of his birth in Bethlehem, or his descent from David.

That it is difficult to account for his being born in Bethlehem is not an objection to it but rather an argument in its favor. One wonders how he could have been born there, if his parents lived in Nazareth. Luke, of course, tries to account for this, but his explanation leads to greater difficulties. But his statement that there was no room for them at the inn, and so the birth took place in a stable, and Jesus was first laid in a manger instead of a cradle, sounds highly historical, as there is no Old Testament prophecy corresponding to either fact, and so likely to have given rise to such a tale.

Later devotion thought angels must have sung above his manger, and astrologers must have offered him gifts and homage, a symbol that their day was done—ways of conveying their sense of the real greatness, the sublimity of what was so quietly and obscurely happening, and of all the help and happiness it really portended for mankind. This is why we can never outgrow Christmas. To us, it all seems understatement!

Historical research has naturally tried to make everything as easy as possible for Joseph and Mary, but that is not always the way things happen in this world, and truth is sometimes stranger than fiction. So there is really no serious argument to be brought against the twofold evidence that Jesus was born in Bethlehem, in the days of Herod the Great, probably in the last days of his reign, which ended in 4 B.C.

In Matthew's story of the virgin birth of Jesus the idea of his divine sonship is translated into narrative form. The Jewish mind instinctively cast its doctrines in the form of narrative. But while the manner of the story is clearly Jewish—the casting of dogma into narrative—the subject matter of it is just as definitely Greek; Greek legend was full of demigods—sons begotten by Zeus, with human mothers. It was a way of stating Jesus' divine sonship in terms intelligible and acceptable to the Greek mind. And to this day many people cannot think of his sonship in any other way. But while Luke takes a very similar view of his birth, our earliest sources, Mark and Paul, show no knowledge of it, and Matthew and Luke are not consistent about it, as both of them trace Jesus' ancestry through Joseph to David.

Certainly he belonged to the tribe of Judah, the one great faithful tribe, which had clung through all the centuries to the house of David, and to the little town which had been his home. That town the prophet Micah had said would again produce the ideal leader and ruler of the Jewish people.

The long reign of Herod, the Edomite adventurer, who with the aid of the Romans had in 39-37 B.C. made himself king of Palestine, was drawing to a close. He had brought law and order to turbulent Palestine and rebuilt its cities and even the temple itself, doubtless in the Greek style then in fashion. But he had done it all as a vassal of the Roman Empire, and personally had been so cruel and brutal that he had put to death two of his own sons, and even their mother, his favorite wife, a descendant of those Maccabean heroes who a century and a half before had freed Palestine from subjection to Syria and made it for one century at least a free and independent state once more. Herod had definite plans for the succession to his throne; he had not spared his own sons when he suspected that they had designs upon it, and what he would do to an outsider with even the remotest suspicion of such ambitions may be imagined.

Ten years after Herod's death his son Archelaus, to whom as governor he had left Judea, had become so intolerable to his subjects that the emperor was obliged to dismiss him and send him into exile. He was replaced as governor by a series of Roman procurators, the fifth of whom was Pontius Pilate, who came out to the province in A.D. 26 and held the post for ten momentous years.

Galilee and Perea (Trans-Jordan) fell at Herod's death

to Herod Antipas as governor. He was, like Archelaus, the son of Herod and Malthace, and he ruled his district until A.D. 37. It was he who took the life of John the Baptist, and through the machinations of the Pharisees in Galilee threatened that of Jesus as well.

A third son of Herod, Herod Philip (by another wife, Cleopatra of Jerusalem), became on the death of Herod governor of a group of districts north and east of the Sea of Galilee—Batanea, Iturea, Trachonitis, and Gaulanitis— which he ruled from 4 B.C. until his death in A.D. 34. Like his father and brother he was fond of building, and rebuilt Caesarea Philippi and Bethsaida Julias into Greek cities. His wife was Salome, the daughter of Herodias.

These were the lands Jesus chiefly frequented, and the men who ruled them in his day.

Matthew says that Joseph took his family to Nazareth to live to escape the possible cruelty of Archelaus, but Luke indicates that both Mary and Joseph were residents of Nazareth before their marriage and returned there to live immediately after Jesus' birth and presentation in the temple. Mark and Paul throw no light on the problem thus created.

But Jesus grew up in Nazareth, then a town of little importance, which lies six hours' horseback ride from the present port of Haifa, and about the same distance from Tiberias and the Sea of Galilee. Nazareth was only two or three miles from Gath-Hepher, the modern El-Meshhed, where the prophet Jonah had lived eight centuries before. Over the hills to the north, three miles away, was Sepphoris, destroyed by the Romans but rebuilt in Jesus' time by Herod Antipas, who made it the capital and the largest town in Galilee.

Jesus' father Joseph was a carpenter, and Jesus when he grew up seems to have followed the same trade. He had brothers and sisters—four brothers, James, Joseph, Judah and Simon, and a number of sisters, who were living in Nazareth when he once preached there in the course of his ministry. So he grew up in a large family. His position as eldest naturally encouraged in him his gift of leadership. His father attended the synagogue and took his part in the worship, as a man of Israel. The children went with their mother and sat with the women, listening. But when Jesus was twelve he was, like other Jewish boys, admitted to a man's part in the service and took his place with the men of Israel.

In the weekly service of the synagogue he heard the Law read aloud in Hebrew, thirty or thirty-five verses every Sabbath, and then immediately translated verse by verse into Aramaic, which was his native tongue. In this way the whole Law, Genesis to Deuteronomy, was covered every three or three and a half years. It was in fact divided into very definite sections for this purpose, each a little longer than one page or one chapter of a modern English Bible. An eager listener could not fail to learn a good deal of Hebrew in this way, as the languages were very much alike.

The Pharisaic Judaism which prevailed in Galilee accepted as scripture the Law—that is, what we know as the

five books of Moses, from Genesis to Deuteronomy—the
Prophets, and the Psalms. But their prophets included the
books of Joshua, Judges, Samuel and Kings—the "Former
Prophets,"—and the "Latter Prophets"—Isaiah, Jeremiah,
Ezekiel and the scroll of the twelve Minor Prophets, as we
call them, by reason of their brevity; the whole twelve
would not bulk as large as Isaiah alone. Jesus sometimes
speaks of the scriptures as "the Law and the Prophets."
As for the book of Psalms, it was the hymnbook and the
prayer book of Jewish people. Jesus once asked his critics
whether they had never read about the stone that the
builders rejected—referring to Psalm 118.

Certainly Jesus knew the Law, the Prophets and the
Psalms. He quotes from them or alludes to them on numerous occasions, and discusses them, when called upon to do
so, with familiarity and penetration. The noble account of
marriage in Genesis, the stories of Abraham and Lot, and
Lot's wife, of David and his adventures, of Solomon and
his splendor, of the prophets Elijah and Elisha, of Isaiah
and his disappointment and his disciples, of Hosea, of
Jonah and the Ninevites, of Jeremiah's new covenant, or
agreement—it must be plain that Jesus could read the
Hebrew scriptures, and did so, with a profound understanding and appreciation of them. They have never had
such a reader!

Just how he learned to read Hebrew, for the Aramaic
translation of them was not yet written down, we can only
conjecture. But a boy as capable as Jesus could easily have
done so simply from listening closely to the weekly reading

of them in the synagogue and their immediate translation into Aramaic, and many lesser men have learned to read under circumstances much more unfavorable. On a later visit to Nazareth, in the course of his ministry, Jesus had no difficulty in finding the place he sought in the long scroll of Isaiah and reading the great oracle on the mission of the Servant of the Lord. Philo of Alexandria declares (about A.D. 40) that the Jews learned to read their scriptures from childhood, and Josephus (about A.D. 90) says young Jews knew their laws as well as they knew their own names. While these may be patriotic exaggerations, they agree astonishingly well with the evidence the gospels give about Jesus.

When he reached the age of twelve, and was ready to sit in the synagogue with his father among the men of Israel, Jesus' parents thought it was time to take him with them up to Jerusalem for the spring feast of the Passover. The noble city, the center of his people's faith and hopes, and the temple, the very house of God himself, made a deep impression upon the active mind of the boy, and on the day set for departure for home after the week of the festival, he made his way again to the temple and was soon absorbed in listening to the scribes and teachers who frequented the magnificent courts and colonnades that Herod had built. His parents meanwhile, in full reliance upon his ability to take care of himself, set out with some little caravan of other pilgrims on their journey home. It was not until nightfall that they observed his absence, and turned back in some anxiety to look for him in Jerusalem.

A day was spent in the return and the search but it was not until next morning that they found him at last, in the temple, listening to the teachers as they expounded the scriptures, and asking them questions. To his mother's reproaches for the anxiety he had caused them, he only replied,

"How did you come to look for me? Did you not know that I must be at my Father's?"

They should have come to the temple first, he thought; where else in the city could he be expected to be found? For was not God his Father, and the temple his Father's house?

This idea of God must have come to him from the prophets and psalmists, and he had found it wonderfully congenial. Hosea had said they were to be sons of the living God (1:10). Jeremiah too had uttered it long before: "I have become a Father to Israel" (31:9). Malachi had said, "Have we not all one Father? Did not one God create us?" And one of the Psalmists had written, "As a father is kind to his children, so the Lord is kind to those who revere him" (103:13). David's great prayer in I Chronicles 29 begins, "Blessed art thou, O Lord God of Israel, our Father for ever and ever." Greek religious thought was coming to this great idea of God the Father of us all, as Epictetus half a century later shows, but it had long been present, though not conspicuously, in the Hebrew religion, in which Jesus was brought up. It is striking that he already felt this designation of God to be the most appealing and satisfying to his religious life. It was indeed to be the key to his message and the keynote of his career.

It was not that he must be about his Father's business that would have guided them at once to the temple; that might have taken him anywhere. It was that he would of course be found at his Father's house. They should, he felt, have known just where to look for him.

Our ancient records leave the biographer of Jesus with a gap of some twenty years of absolute silence, of which they say nothing. This has led some imaginative people to fill in the period with fanciful journeys and studies, of little real service to the task of understanding Jesus and his message. We may be sure he did a world of thinking in those busy years of working at his trade in Nazareth. He must indeed have nourished a youth sublime with the messages of the prophets, especially Isaiah, whom he knew so well and who so clearly influenced him at various stages of his work. And he surveyed the life about him, with its joys and sorrows, its pains and wrongs, with extraordinary keenness and sympathy.

The family in which Jesus grew up was evidently an earnestly religious one, but sharp divisions arose in it very early. Jesus' brother James was evidently a strong character, who found his satisfactions in what we know as Pharisaic religion—that devotion to the observances of the Mosaic Law as interpreted and defined in detail by the scribes. It was he who came forward after Jesus' death, as the heir of his position, and for a time was in fact the head of the Jerusalem church. Indeed, he was in a fair way to make the Christian movement, in Jerusalem at least, little

more than a new form of Pharisaism, when he encountered the strong opposition of the apostle Paul, who had
been a thorough Pharisee in his youth and had seen the
hollowness of it. It was this narrow attitude that made the
Jerusalem church soon take a second place to the church
at Antioch, which James did not control. And yet James
eventually became a martyr of the new movement, being
stoned to death, Josephus reports, some ten years later.

This division over religion in his home is reflected in
the fact that Jesus did not find, or apparently look for, his
first followers among his brothers and sisters, but among
some fishermen he had met and made friends with at
John's outdoor meetings down on the banks of the Jordan.
Jesus evidently knew that his great new consciousness of a
divine commission would find no encouragement in his
own home circle in Nazareth; as he afterward said, he had
come to turn a man against his father, and a daughter
against her mother, and a man's enemies would be in his
own household. But of course the decisive proof of this is
the behavior of his mother and his brothers after he had
begun to preach in and about Capernaum. They said he
was out of his senses, and went up to Capernaum to try
to stop him.

So Jesus' youth was probably one of dawning and in-
creasing dissatisfaction with the prevalent form of the
Jewish religion in Nazareth and in his own home. He did
not in those early years see what he could do about it, but
he must have felt a growing sense that there was something
deeply wrong about it, which should be corrected.

CHAPTER II

His Great Vocation Bursts upon Him

It was the fifteenth year of the reign of Tiberius, the year we speak of as A.D. 28-29 (for the ancient year began not with the first of January but with the twenty-ninth of August), when a great prophet suddenly appeared in the wild country that lay east of Judea along the shores of the Dead Sea. He was the sensation of the day. He revived Amos' message of a dreadful day of wrath and punishment for an unrepentant world. He lived the life of a hermit, eating raw food, wearing rough clothes, keeping away from towns and settlements. His manner of life stamped him as a prophet and irresistibly reminded people of Elijah, the fiery old desert prophet of nine centuries before, who had worn a hairy mantle, taken refuge in caves, and been fed by ravens.

John's vehement demand for repentance and obedience to the will of God soon created an immense impression. People streamed out to his camp meetings, as we would call them, and listened spellbound to his message. They soon identified him as a returned Elijah, come back to earth as Malachi had foretold, to be God's messenger, sent to warn mankind and prepare them for the coming of the terrible day of the Lord. In the boldest terms he warned the Jews who came in crowds to hear him that their descent from Abraham meant nothing to God compared with a life of helpfulness to others, with whom they must share their food and clothing. Even tax collectors, who made their living by padding their tax rolls, and soldiers, notorious as extortioners and informers, asked him what they must do. He told them bluntly that they must reform, and warned them all that someone greater than he was soon to come to institute a Messianic judgment and punish those who failed to repent and reform.

But his sternest rebuke was called forth, Matthew says, by the appearance in his wilderness audiences of people he recognized as from the dominant religious sects, the Pharisees and Sadducees. The Sadducees were dominant in and about Jerusalem, the Pharisees more generally throughout the land. Who had warned this brood of snakes, he bitingly inquired, to escape the wrath that was coming? If they were going to confess their sins and profess repentance, they had better show their sincerity in a complete change of conduct. For the descent from Abraham on which they so strongly relied counted for nothing in the sight of God. Why, he could raise up descendants for Abraham right out of the very stones that covered the ground at their feet. This was striking right at the doctrine of national religious privilege that was the cornerstone of Judaism. But the time was short; the ax was already lying at the roots of the trees, and any tree that failed to produce good fruit was going to be cut down and burned.

Jewish visitors from western provinces joined the crowds that went out to hear him, and carried his message back to cities like Ephesus, where Paul twenty-five or thirty years later found groups of John's disciples. Jesus did not hesitate to call John the greatest man who had ever lived, and actually accepted baptism at his hands, the rite of purification in token of repentance which John demanded of his followers.

Baptism was an ancient rite of Judaism. It was part of the Levitical purification prescribed in ridding oneself of certain types of impurity, as in Leviticus 14:9, Numbers 19:7, 8, and so on. It had also been adopted in the Jewish mission as one of the three demands made upon Jewish proselytes, or converts, from other peoples and religions, when they entered the Jewish fold—circumcision, baptism, and a sacrifice. It was also in use in Mithraism, as an initiatory purification, but it was the Jewish rite which John signalized as the symbol of repentance and spiritual purification. He baptized his penitents in token of their repentance. The early gospels say nothing of its use by Jesus; but Paul speaks of its occasional use in his churches, it is definitely expected of converts to Christianity in the Acts and it is a part of the ministry of Jesus, though practiced only by his disciples, in John. But it was evidently John the Baptist who had exalted it to the status of a symbol of the determination to lead a better life. It was that, of course, that had given him his title; he was the Baptizer.

John does not seem to have had any organization,

though the seed he sowed in his preaching along the Jordan was carried far over the ancient world. But his rite of baptism sent his followers forth not just momentarily swayed toward a better life but, in their own minds at least, publicly committed, by accepting it, to a higher course of conduct. It was the symbol of a decision reached and acted upon, a public commitment to the abandonment of old sins and the entrance upon a new life. And while John seems to have made no effort to organize his followers, it is clear that many of them organized themselves into Johannist circles out in the great centers of the Roman world, far beyond the limits of Palestine.

But what gave John's baptism everlasting significance was its effect upon Jesus. Jesus had joined the throngs of earnest, serious inquirers for the will of God who trudged off to John's meetings in the wilderness. The two men were cousins, born within a few months of each other, and probably had known each other at least slightly from boyhood. John's father Zechariah belonged to the priesthood and went up to Jerusalem once a year to take his turn in the priestly functions. But there was nothing priestly about John; his affinities were all with the prophets, and the old heroic figures of Amos, Elijah and Malachi seemed to live again in him. He revived the old prophetic view of religion as a life of uprightness in the sight of God, regardless of legalism and ritual, and enforced it with terrible pictures of judgment, wrath and punishment to come, unless men would repent and obey.

Jesus' religious life had awakened early. From boyhood

he had learned to think of himself, as Hosea had said, as a son of the Living God. He had certainly nourished a youth sublime with the searching, stirring oracles of his people's prophets, particularly Hosea and Isaiah. He must have been among the first to answer his cousin's call, and hastened to join him. So it is as a disciple of John that Jesus first appears in history. He was probably one of the closer, perhaps the inner circle of them, for he afterward spoke of John as the new Elijah foretold by Malachi, and accepted him as his own herald and forerunner.

So it must have been very soon after news of John's work reached Nazareth that Jesus, a carpenter about thirty years of age, set forth with a little caravan of people attracted by what they had heard of John's personality and message. His passion to do everything God required would make him one of the first to hasten to his cousin's banner. He found him somewhere on the banks of the lower Jordan, already surrounded by crowds of people, half-curious, half-serious. Jesus was soon satisfied that John's message expressed the will of God and pressed forward for baptism in the turbid waters of the muddy river.

It was a sublime moment in his life. For as he came up out of the water, serene in the consciousness that he was doing his utmost to carry out the will of God, a tremendous sense of vocation, selection and mission came over him. He heard a voice saying to him,

"You are my Son, my Beloved! You are my Chosen!"

He felt filled with the Spirit of God, as never before. For an instant, the heavens had opened, and the Spirit had taken possession of him. A curtain had rolled up in his mind and he saw with a new and surpassing clearness what God really wanted life to be and the great role God intended him to play in the drama of redemption. In such visions God had called Isaiah and Jeremiah to their work as prophets.

In after days he described it with his imperial imagination to his closest followers in his own unmistakable gigantesque, that inimitable quality which, Chesterton pointed out, stamps his most characteristic utterances. He saw the heavens torn open and the Spirit coming down like a dove, to take possession of him. It was doubtless the climax of much religious reflection and experience, but it was none the less the great moment, the decisive hour, not only in Jesus' life but in human experience. One man had at last been caught up as no one before into the vision of God, to be his spokesman, his Chosen, his Beloved, his Son.

This was an immensely uplifting and inspiring experience, but it was also an appalling and perplexing one. Under this new conviction, to which he had now given himself up, Jesus fled from the crowds of people that thronged about John and hurried away, driven by the Spirit, as he put it, into more solitary parts of the region for a time of reflection, as he grappled with his task and mission. After weeks of solitary wrestling that engrossed his whole mind and soul, most of the time forgetful of food and drink, he fell from his tremendous exaltation into a mood of deep depression, which he regarded as temptation.

The gospels tell of it in his own unmistakable language, just as he afterward related it to his disciples. If he was indeed God's Son, could he not make the stones at his feet, that to his imagination looked so like the cakes of bread he so much needed, actually turn to bread, to satisfy his hunger? But bread was not his greatest need! In imagination he saw himself in the temple at Jerusalem; if he was God's Chosen could he not by some one spectacular act, casting himself from a pinnacle to be borne up in their hands by the angels, command the obedience and worship of the Jewish people who gathered there? But a voice within him answered, You shall not try the Lord your God! Last of all, he saw himself carried away to the summit of a mountain so high that from it he could see all the kingdoms of the world in their splendor. A little compromise, a little yielding to the tempter's demands, and all these could be his own. How far could he relax his demands and yet carry out his great task? He could not relax them at all! He would be the one religious leader who never compromised.

"Begone, Satan," he cried. "The Scripture says, You must do homage to the Lord your God and worship him alone!"

With this decision a great relief swept over him, and as he must have put it to his disciples, telling them later of this experience, the devil left him, and angels came and waited on him.

CHAPTER III

The First Disciples

It is altogether probable that the interruption of John's work took place while Jesus was going through his solitary experience of reflection and adjustment after his great baptismal experience, with its overwhelming conviction of divine commission. Jesus returned to the scene of John's activities to find his crowds of hearers dispersed to their homes and to learn the terrible news that John himself was in prison. The opening for which he was naturally looking, to begin his own work, was thus plain before him. He went back to Galilee whence he had come a few weeks before, not, however, to his own town of Nazareth, but to the western shores of the Sea of Galilee, so densely peopled in his day that they are still strewn all the way from one end of the lake to the other with the massive remains of first-century buildings.

For Jesus had no idea of burying himself in solitude as John had done, and waiting for people to come to him. He went to them, and sought them out. The ministry of preaching into which he now threw himself carried him far and wide about Galilee and the neighboring country. Not only his method but his message was in strong contrast to John's. From the first Jesus proclaimed the kingdom of heaven, the reign of God on earth. He declared as John had done that men must repent and prepare for it, but Jesus announced it not as doom but as good news. He preached a gospel, in which men must believe. He invited them to share in the joy and blessing of the kingdom he proclaimed. It was to bring men happiness, not misery. He foresaw a fuller, better life for those who would accept his message.

Jesus did not declare himself to be the Messiah of Jewish expectation; that title was too likely to be misunderstood, and would have attracted to him a horde of Zealots, nationalists and revolutionaries who would have cared little for his moral and religious teaching. The word which in Hebrew means simply "anointed," that is, as rightful king of the Davidic line, as in the Psalms, had been employed in a variety of senses, in Daniel and the Book of Enoch.

Some have imagined that Jesus first went home to Nazareth, but this is most unlikely. Mark says nothing of such a return home. And what we know of the attitude of Jesus' family to his religious work makes it seem very improbable. We soon find them declaring that he is beside himself and out of his right mind, and doing their best to stop him, and the earliest gospels give us no reason to think they ever changed their minds about him, until after his death. His subsequent activity makes it clear that Jesus would have found no encouragement at home had he turned thither after his great experience in the wilderness.

So when he found John gone and his meetings broken up, Jesus turned first to the friends he had made among John's disciples, especially some Galileans who had gathered about him in the course of John's meetings.

The western shore of the Sea of Galilee was in Jesus' day a flourishing, thickly populated district, certainly all the way from Tiberias to Capernaum. Along its shores Jesus made his way northward, as an outdoor preacher, declaring that the time predicted by prophets like Daniel and Malachi had come, and the reign of God on earth, the climax of Jewish hopes, was to begin. Among the fishermen along the shore were men whom he had met before among John's hearers at the Jordan; probably he had come in search of them. He and they were not strangers to one another and he wished first to tell them of his tremendous new experience. It is striking that he does not first go home to Nazareth, to his brothers and sisters. Plainly the spiritual companionships he had formed at John's meetings he had found and still felt a closer bond than that of home. Along the shores of that beautiful lake he sought out the men he had come to know and value in the camps of John's eager listeners in the wilderness, to renew that religious fellowship and summon them to share his great enterprise.

John had preached repentance in preparation for the divine day of judgment which he believed to be imminent. But Jesus sees in God's dawning reign not a threat but a promise. Its coming is good news, which men must believe, and prepare for by repentance. This simple fact is obvious in the very word *gospel* and yet is often overshadowed by condemnation and dire threats of punishment. But as Jesus preached it, it was a thing to be hoped for and eagerly desired, not dreaded but welcomed.

Not only his message but his way of presenting it was very unlike John's. John had retired to the wilderness to preach to those who made the long journey to hear him. Jesus hastened into Galilee, the most settled region of Palestine, to carry his message directly to the people of the land. Jesus himself came from Galilee, for Nazareth was a town of Galilee, and his first appearance, as far as we know, after his return from the wilderness, was no more than a day's walk from there. Perhaps he had begun to preach already, but his first action of which we know was to find his old associates and summon them to his aid.

They had returned from John's meetings to their old haunts and labors, as fishermen in the Sea of Galilee. Their homes were in Capernaum, a flourishing town at the northwest corner of the lake, adjoining the fertile plain of Gennesaret, after which the lake was sometimes called the Lake of Gennesaret (Luke 5:1).

He espied them out in their boat, casting their nets for the fish with which the lake abounded.

"Come, follow me," he cried to them, "and I will make you fish for men!"

They must have known him already for the natural leader he was, for they did not hesitate, but abandoned their nets and their boat, and joined him on his way.

It was a momentous beginning, for one of them, Simon, was an extraordinary personality, and was destined in a few months to stand forth as the leader of Jesus' movement and to prove a heroic and gifted figure. He would have his moments of weakness, indeed, but his amazing personality was to carry Jesus' movement through its most trying and perilous time. It was no ordinary fisherman whom Jesus enlisted that day on the shores of Galilee. Men came afterward to think of him as the chief of the apostles.

The three men went on along the shore to where another pair of fishermen were in their boat at work on their nets, with their father Zebedee. They were James and John. They too must have been old companions of John's camp meetings, on whom Jesus felt he could rely and who had shown their attachment to him. He called them too, and, like Simon and Andrew, they had no hesitation in obeying his summons. How far it was going to carry them all, they could have had no idea. Enough that he wanted them. They were ready and glad to go with him, not stopping to ask whether it was for a day or a month; probably they did not think beyond that time. And of these four, three were to be his closest confidants, his inner circle from that moment to the end of his ministry.

From them, too, was to come to later ages the clearest picture of what he was, and what he tried to do. For it was Simon's memories of what he said and what he did in the months that followed that were to give mankind, all of us, our most intimate knowledge of him. But of that tremendous drama that was about to unfold before and around them the four fishermen could have had no idea. They were on the eve of a great experience which would

raise them far above themselves and their old companions
and make them partners in a sublime enterprise and in the
fullest sense heroes of a new era for mankind. All of this
the result of hearing and accompanying the young man of
thirty who had called them to the shore, of following him
and obeying him.

They went on together to Capernaum, where Simon
and Andrew lived, and probably James and John did too.
Then or soon after Jesus must have told them of his new
experience and all that it had led to, and of the work that
now lay before him, in which he wanted their companionship and help. They were to be his partners in the enterprise. For like the prophets of old and probably like John
the Baptist in his own day, Jesus wanted a group of disciples, to live with and talk with and teach. Isaiah had had
such a circle, and Jeremiah's disciple and secretary,
Baruch, was probably the man who had preserved and
edited the records of Jeremiah's work and preaching.

Jesus went home to Capernaum with them; from now
on he was to make his home with one or another of his followers. At Capernaum it was probably with Simon. In
talks with his four friends he must have told of all that had
happened to him since their last meeting, at John's revival
in the wilderness: of his tremendous experience at his
baptism, the heavens opening and the Spirit of God sweeping down into his heart, and of the inner voice that told
him of his great role and God's purpose for him—God's
Son, his Beloved, his Chosen! Chosen to proclaim and set

up the reign of God in the hearts of men. It was to be not a condemnation, as the prophets had thought, but an invitation, to welcome the spirit of God into their hearts and live in the assurance of his forgiveness, his care and his love—yes, and of his presence too within them.

On the Sabbath they went to the synagogue, and given an opportunity to speak, Jesus gave this as his message. It was no mere appeal to the old written Law, no effort to interpret it and enforce it, such as they were accustomed to hear from the scribes and Pharisees, but an authoritative appeal, independent of it, to a new life of harmony and fellowship with God; his spirit in their hearts, if they admitted him, would direct them and show them how to carry out his will.

This made a deep impression. But he was interrupted in his address by a loud outcry from a demoniac—a poor fellow mentally deranged and emotionally unstable who broke in upon him, crying out in fear and anger.

"What do you want of us, Jesus, you Nazarene?" He shouted. "Have you come to destroy us? I know who you are, you are God's holy One."

In Jesus' day most forms of sickness, physical or mental, were popularly dismissed as the work of demons who took possession of people. Sometimes one, sometimes seven, sometimes a whole legion of them, would take possession of a man or woman. And of course if you are sick, and everyone around you thinks you are possessed with a devil, very soon you will begin to think so too and exhibit the usual symptoms. It would be hard for most of us to retain our sanity, for instance, if everybody thought we were insane, and said so.

Jesus had no patience with the man's delusion.

"Silence," he cried. "Get out of him."

This confident appeal to the man's deeper nature dispelled his pitiful illusion and brought him to his senses. With a farewell shriek the demon, as he considered it, went out of him.

The people in the synagogue were amazed and perplexed. What could it mean? Accustomed as they were to the prevalent legalism of the Pharisees who dominated popular religion, they seemed to hear in his teaching a new note. And this bold defiance of the demon in their midst filled them with wonder:

"He gives orders with authority even to the foul spirits, and they obey him!"

This was the beginning of a widespread publicity for Jesus all over Galilee.

There was no little excitement, we may believe, as his four disciples escorted Jesus home from the synagogue, to the house of Simon and Andrew. There Simon's mother-in-law had taken to her bed with a fever, of the intermittent kind still prevalent about the lake, and Jesus was told of it. He went up to her bedside and helped her to her feet. The fever left her, and she went about her household duties. This was the kind of thing Jesus was constantly doing, so much so that it became the one thing everybody knew about him—that he could cure the sick and drive

out the demons. The earliest gospel is full of such incidents, and we cannot doubt that such things did happen.
When people tried to thank him, he would say,

"It is your faith that has saved you!"

With such contagious faith in the goodness and the
power of God and his own convincing good will and kindness of heart, certainly one of his leading traits, he also
roused in them the will to health and sanity and life,
always such a reinforcement and often even a necessity
to any cure.

The news of this spread rapidly through the town and
over the countryside, and right after sunset, when the
Sabbath day was over, people brought their sick and
demon-possessed to Simon's house for Jesus' aid; the whole
town seemed to have gathered at Simon's door, and again
Jesus helped and cured them. The truth is, nothing about
the early ministry of Jesus is plainer than that it was
chiefly as a wonder-worker, a benefactor and doer of good
to people in physical or mental distress that he was first
known. This gift of his impressed the simple people about
him far more than his religious message, and even dis-
tracted their minds from it—so much so that soon he felt
obliged to instruct the people he cured to say nothing
about it, but keep the fact to themselves. But that he did
such things on many occasions colors almost every page of
the earliest gospel and remains a striking evidence of his
great desire to relieve the physical as well as the moral
misery he saw about him. A great consciousness of the
needs of the people about him had come over him. His was

no ivory tower, in which he would take refuge from the common woes of men. Rather, he went about doing good. This was no pose, no adjunct external to his main work of preaching; it was a deep compassion, the very love and mercy of God, finding expression through him. What other source can they have had?

> 'Tis God himself becomes apparent, when
> God's wisdom and God's goodness are display'd,

as Saint Bernard said, and Matthew Arnold after him.

"The miracles of which Mark is so full," says Montefiore (*Synoptic Gospels,* I, 306), "leave us cold. Of them we have nothing to learn." Impossible not to be moved at the sight of a man so stirred with compassion and good will for his miserable fellow-men, so eager to help them whatever their distresses, and so capable of doing so! A man who went all over Galilee doing them good and nothing but good, physical and spiritual, and all without stopping to ask, in the spirit of Leviticus 26 or Deuteronomy 28, whether they were absolutely upright and without sins of any kind! That is to take a purely dogmatic view of all this compassion and ask how valid all these stories are as "signs," as the Pharisees put it. But Jesus said he would not give them any signs, of hands turned leprous, or sticks turned into snakes. Yet they were signs, indeed, but in a very different sense from theirs. For is there anything men want so much to find out about God as whether he really cares about them and their weaknesses and woes? The

Gospel of Mark is the great answer to that question, as the curtain rises on the kingdom of God.

Luke is the only one of our ancient sources to give us light on how the life and work of Jesus are to be fitted into the chronology of his times. Luke says that when Jesus began his work he was about thirty years of age (3:23). If John's work began in A.D. 28-29, the fifteenth year of the reign of Tiberius (Luke 3:1), and Jesus came to hear him soon after, say in the autumn, and John's arrest took place soon after Jesus' baptism, and Jesus began to preach almost immediately after John's arrest, Jesus must have begun his work at the earliest toward the end of A.D. 28, and if he was born in 4 B.C. he would then be thirty-one or thirty-two. This would limit the time of his active ministry to little more than six months.

Many people find satisfaction in the view that Jesus was just another prophet, like one of the prophets. He certainly had much in common with them. But his unfailing devotion to helping his fellow-men, and women and children, the sick, the blind, the lame, the mad, the fearful, the miserable, of every kind, which the oldest gospel represents as his leading trait, marks him as supremely a doer of the will of God. This was no advertising campaign, to attract hearers for his message, but an irresistible overflowing of love and good will and compassion for the sheer misery of mankind, a revelation of God's own attitude, which was not vindictive and judicial but full of pity and forgiveness. This is the supreme meaning of Jesus' won-

ders: God's will of mercy and salvation was expressing
itself through him. And there is certainly nothing about
God that men need and want more to know than precisely
this! Is he, they ask themselves, really not a harsh judge
but a loving and understanding Father? Jesus' every action
answered that question. Even when it embarrassed his
preaching of his message, he could not forbear to help the
poor creatures about him.

The prophets were men who saw the coming of the
kingdom of God afar off. They envisioned it chiefly as a
dreadful day of judgment, when the wicked would get the
punishment that was due them. As Zephaniah said, "A day
of wrath is that day!" And while Hosea lifted up his voice
for the love of God, the prophets in general viewed the day
of the Lord as a fearful prospect. The kingdom of God, too,
they assigned to the distant future. Even John the Baptist
still pushed it into the future. But Jesus declared it had
come. The time was fulfilled—it was up; it had come—for
the reign of God to be set up on earth, and he was the
agent, the commissioner for that great undertaking.

And how true it was! The kingdom of God was at their
doors. They had only to enter into it, and live as though it
was present. This is what forever marks Jesus off from the
prophets. He realized and proclaimed that it was here! You
have only to live in it, accept its laws and ways, and the
felicity the prophets dreamed of will be yours.

So Jesus stands apart from the prophets, with whom he
has so much in common, in this great disclosure: the time

has come, the reign of God is among you; repent and believe this good news.

For Jesus knew that its good news far outweighed its menace, of punishment and destruction. His faith in God was such, and his conviction of God's goodness and love was such, that he knew the reign of God in men's hearts on earth meant far more of happiness, usefulness and joy than of penalty and punishment. His own life was a supreme illustration of what life in the kingdom of God could be, for it was overflowing with ministries of good will and helpfulness to all about him. He lived the gospel that he taught, and men sometimes wonder which outweighed the other, his life or his teaching.

Most of us are hardly equal to our own private griefs and burdens, but Jesus boldly took upon himself the burdens of all about him. He evidently felt that it was wrong to pass by any scene of suffering that he could relieve, without relieving it. Far from using this to advertise his mission, he tried to get the people he helped to say nothing about it, but they persisted in reporting what he had done for them, and his reputation as a wonder-worker threatened to eclipse what he regarded as his real work, of preaching repentance, and the presence of the kingdom of God. Very soon he found it impossible to visit towns at all, and had to stay out in unfrequented places, where people seriously interested would seek him out and hear his preaching.

CHAPTER IV

Jesus Begins His Work in Galilee

In the earliest gospel, again and again, we behold a scene of distress and grief; Jesus comes on the stage, and immediately says something or does something to relieve and remedy the situation. He is presented to us not so much as a teacher, but as a doer, a man of action, whose first impulse when he saw people in distress or need was to help them out, a tremendous index of his character. He loved them, impoverished, demon-possessed and disease-ridden as they were; a great compassion seized him, and he brought them out of their distresses. From the beginning of his work to the end, nothing is more characteristic of him than this, for finally he died for them.

So we do not shrink from his mighty works; they are the most important, the supreme index of the great passion of his life, to help and save his fellow-men. Without them, or the record of them, he might appear a mere teacher, simply pointing men to a better way; but he was more than that. Every need of theirs appealed to him, and called forth a response. He was already possessed by the spirit of that great oracle in Isaiah about preaching the good news to the poor, releasing the prisoners, giving sight to the blind, and setting the downtrodden free.

So from the very outset of his ministry Jesus displayed that real and deep concern for the personal needs of men and women that has made him ever since the symbol of such helpfulness and sympathy. Yet this new power to attract and interest and benefit the common people about him gave Jesus no little anxiety. His host in Capernaum observed that he got up long before morning, and went off by himself to a lonely place to pray. How was he to use this rising popularity wisely and effectively? In the morning his new disciples, Simon at their head, followed him and found him, to tell him that everybody was looking for him. His fame as a wonder-worker had begun; that was why they were looking for him. They wanted to see the man who had cured them the night before, and perhaps witness further wonders from him.

From this prospect Jesus turned away, without explanation. He said to them,

"Let us go somewhere else, to the neighboring towns, so that I may preach in them too, for that is why I came out here."

He had left the house to avoid just the situation that had developed, and to be ready to move on, to tell his message in other places as he had already done in Capernaum. His preaching must have precedence over his curing the sick.

And now began that strange pilgrimage of Jesus with his faithful four, among the towns of populous, flourishing Galilee.

Some moderns decry Mark's gospel as poorly written and choppy in style, because he passes rapidly, without pausing to draw a moral or preach a sermon in each incident, from one scene to another with breathless speed. And yet how influential his work was! It initiated the whole gospel-writing movement, and formed the chief narrative source of both Matthew and Luke. And by itself it commands the attention of the modern historian more than either of the later gospels.

Mark derived these brief narratives, as we have seen, from the preaching of Peter, away in Rome a generation after Jesus' death, and no doubt Peter made full use of their homiletical values. Peter himself, as the stories abundantly show, had some of the old Hebrew genius for storytelling that meets us in the narratives of the Old Testament. Their very crispness and brevity make a strong appeal. And their swift sequence of one upon another produces on the reader a strange effect. Was there no limit to this man's patience and sympathy? He seems to go on and on, day after day, and case after case, curing, helping, saving one man, woman or child after another, until it dawns upon us that this is the boundless mercy and love of God that is being shown, welling up in inexhaustible fullness in the heart of Jesus. Mark hardly speaks of it, but he does not need to. He has shown it in a much more effective way.

And since nothing is so interesting as narrative, Mark has written the kind of gospel most likely to lay hold of the Greek public he wrote for. Mere preaching one might forget, or close one's mind to, but these plain tales, so utterly simple and unpretending, interest the reader in spite of himself. They are so short the reader cannot be bored, and so vivid and varied that he is carried along. He is seeing, as Dr. Horton put it, "the Cartoons of St. Mark." Each might in other hands be expanded into a long narrative; of course it has been done. But no one has ever told the stories so effectively as Mark did, following as best he could the words of Peter, as he had heard him tell them to his Roman audiences four or five years before.

In many of the towns Jesus visited, he or his four companions had friends or relatives with whom they could lodge; in others his rising reputation would find entertainment for himself and his companions. As in Capernaum, he preached in the local synagogues, for his message was not hostile to the sound teachings of Judaism, but reinforced them. The great Shema, still the rallying cry of the Jews, with its noble demand that men love God with their whole hearts and souls and with all their might, he declared the first, the great command, and put beside it the words of Leviticus, "You must love your neighbor as you do yourself." He was not for a moment to be thought of as undermining the Law and the Prophets, their great scriptures; he had come not to destroy but to fulfill and enforce them.

But the prevalent religion of Palestine was Pharisaism, which in its devotion to the Law had built a fence around it, and prescribed so many trivial refinements of its precepts as to reduce it to a huge system of minute details of conduct. The result was, the basic attitude of heart was lost in extreme attention to external minutiae. But what Jesus wanted to cure and save was the inner life, and compared with that, externals were of no importance. As Paul put it afterward, "The real Jew is the man who is one inwardly, and receives his praise not from men, but from God."

With this little group of five friends, headed by Jesus, walking about Galilee, preaching, talking and visiting with the people of all kinds, not omitting the despised and neglected "people of the land," as the Jews called them, the Christian movement began. Indeed, one of its most distinctive features was this deep concern for these religious outcasts, who simply could not keep the mass of petty regulations their Pharisaic teachers insisted upon, and to whom in consequence Pharisaism had nothing to offer. But when Jesus looked upon the crowds of people who flocked to hear him, his heart was touched, because they were like sheep that had no shepherd.

Modern American Judaism of the orthodox kind is descended directly from this Pharisaic school, which was the only form of Judaism to survive the destructions of Jerusalem in A.D. 70 and again in A.D. 135. It was in fact designed to enable Judaism to survive any conquest, by maintaining Jewish ways of life so completely that Judaism could never disappear. The Jewish food requirements made it impossible for the Jew to eat familiarly with heathen, whose meats and ways of cooking violated the Jewish law.

A distinguished Jew once told me that in his student days in Berlin he helped himself along by tutoring in a well-to-do Jewish house. Arriving late one Friday night, without his key, he thoughtlessly pressed the button of the doorbell, and was soon admitted to the house. His employers, however, were horrified at what he had done. As the Sabbath had begun, he should not have rung the electric bell, but have knocked. On the Sabbath, he was informed, they never used electric bells, or even electric lights, resorting to candles instead. This is precisely the procedure of Pharisaism, adjusted to modern life. It clothed a host of perfectly harmless acts with what it stigmatized as disobedience to God. The result was a system so elaborate and artificial that common people who had to earn their livings could not keep up with it, and so fell outside the circle of religion. These the Jews dismissed from their minds as "people of the land." As the Pharisees put it, "These common people, who do not know the Law, are doomed!"

In this interest in such religious outcasts, as Dr. Fosdick has recently pointed out, Jesus struck a new note in religion.

For it was to these common people, scattered through the towns of Galilee, that Jesus now began to carry his message of God's love and care, and their right to think of themselves as his children. In doing so of course he disregarded and practically set aside most of the trivial and indifferent detail to which the Pharisees had reduced religion, and recalled those who heard him to a simple but deep trust in God as their Father, whom they must love beyond everything else, and to a life of love for their fellow-men, patience with them, and forgiveness for them. With a religious insight, directness and force which none of the prophets had equaled, he preached this gospel to the unchurched masses of the Galilean countryside, telling them that the time had come when God was going to set up his kingdom in the world, and begin to reign in it, and that reign must now begin in their hearts.

He did not, like the prophets, foretell its coming; he stepped right into the picture and began to set it up. He did not predict it, he began it. He inaugurated it, and undertook to carry out the greatest task ever conceived—to set up the kingdom of God on earth.

CHAPTER V

The First Clash with the Pharisees and the Choosing of the Twelve

After some time spent in thus moving about Galilee, Jesus returned to Capernaum, which he evidently regarded as his home and headquarters. A greater crowd than ever immediately surrounded the door, and some determined people, who wanted his help for a paralytic friend, had to make an opening in the flat roof of the one-story house and lower the sick man on his mattress into Jesus' presence. This is one of the most extraordinary and yet realistic stories in all the record of Jesus' cures. Jesus told the poor fellow that his sins were forgiven. In an age when sickness and misfortune generally were regarded as divine punishment for wrongdoing, this was unexpected and blasphemous. What right had he to forgive the man's sins? Some of the scribes, the professional champions of the Mosaic Law, were sitting about him, listening, and these thoughts at once occurred to them. Jesus saw what they must be thinking, and called upon the sick man to get up, and pick up his mat and go home. And to the amazement of everybody, Mark declares, the man obeyed.

This was the beginning of scribal—that is, Pharisaic—hostility. To claim to forgive sins was going too far. Curing the sick man did not justify or excuse it. They knew or thought they knew of men, rabbis and others, who could heal the sick and cast out demons. But forgiving sins belonged to God alone, except as it could be secured through the priests by means of certain prescribed offerings—Leviticus 4:20, 26, 31, 35; Numbers 15:25, 26, 28, etc. Now Jesus' message coupled forgiveness with repentance. People needed only to repent, to be forgiven. He was proclaiming God's forgiveness. The coming of the day of the Lord meant, for him, not condemnation but forgiveness.

Outside the town again, on the shore of the lake, all the people gathered around him and he taught them. Beside the lake stood the official desk, tollhouse and office of a tax collector, who doubtless collected the petty taxes on the fish that were caught and brought in from the lake. The tax collector was Levi. Jesus saw him sitting there and said to him,

"Follow me!"

The tax collector too must have known him, for he got right up and went with him. Such men were not regarded by the Pharisees as religiously respectable, for they did not hold aloof from contact with heathen and did not attempt to observe the minute details of the Law as the Pharisees defined it. And they were often unprincipled and oppressive besides.

Jesus and his immediate disciples, however, had no scruples about eating with such men as Levi, and that same day or soon after were doing so, apparently at Simon's house, where Jesus was now staying. Levi's joining the movement had led other men of his calling to come in to dine with them, and with them others who made no pretense of observing the rules of the Pharisees. This shocked the legal experts among the Pharisees, and they called the disciples' attention to its impropriety.

"Why does he eat with tax collectors and irreligious people?" they inquired.

When Jesus heard of it, he said to them,

"It is not well people but sick ones who have to have the doctor. I did not come to invite the pious but the irreligious."

This of course led to further criticism of Jesus by the Pharisees, for they were strongly opposed to eating with anyone who did not observe the Law with all their elaborations of it. The legalists regarded people like Levi and his friends as disreputable.

Another ground of objection soon presented itself. The pious Pharisees and even John's disciples, of whom there must have been many in Capernaum, were observing one of the Jewish fasts which were scattered through the year, in July, August, October, January and March. If the fast was for more than one day, Monday and Thursday were the days for its observance, and those who fasted were easily identified by the neglect of their personal appearance and their somber manner and expression. People were quick to observe that Jesus and his group of followers were not observing the fast days, but eating their meals and going about as usual, and they asked him why it was. He replied with one of his penetrating questions.

"Can wedding guests fast when the bridegroom is with them?"

Of course among the Jews a wedding was a time of prolonged feasting—a week, or even two weeks—and merrymaking, as in the case of Tobias and Sarah, in the story of Tobit. Jesus felt that his disciples were in such a mood of joy in their association with him that to take up the practices of a fast simply because of the calendar would be religiously meaningless, and positively hypocritical, for the fast must really reflect one's religious emotions to have any meaning at all. He went on to illustrate this by pointing out the absurdity of sewing a patch of new cloth on an old coat, or putting new wine into old wineskins, for as it ferments it expands and will burst the old skins, which have already been stretched as far as they can be. This was a striking way of suggesting the newness of the religious teaching he had to offer. He plainly thought it was bringing something new into Judaism.

Another thing soon happened that offended the Pharisees. Pushing through the standing grain, on some familiar and recognized footpath through a wheat field, Jesus' disciples, probably unconsciously, broke off some of the heads of wheat, or perhaps they instinctively picked a few as they pushed their way along. To follow such paths even after the wheat was grown was a recognized practice. But to pluck more than three heads of wheat the Pharisees ruled to be an act of reaping, and unlawful on the Sabbath, when work was forbidden by the Law.

The Pharisees were quick to seize upon this trivial incident, and to tax Jesus with it. His disciples, they told him, were breaking the Sabbath law.

He reminded them of what David did when he and his men were in need of food, and took the very Presentation loaves from the altar, which no one but the priests were, under the Law, permitted to eat.

"The Sabbath," he declared, "was made for man, not man for the Sabbath." Human need, always as we have seen so important to the mind of Jesus, was paramount. He does not stop to argue about their trivial legalistics, but strikes to the heart of the institution. Why, of course it was for human need—that of rest—that the Sabbath was instituted; they have inverted its significance. The Law itself for that one day emancipated man and beast, slave and free, from labor (Deuteronomy 5:14). Man—for that is what Son of Man means here, as it does so often (more than ninety times) in Ezekiel, in Daniel 7:13 and sometimes in the Book of Enoch (46:2, 4), where it seems to be on its way to being used of the coming Messiah—man and his needs are supreme over any institution, even one as sacred and ancient as the Sabbath. Jesus frequently spoke of the Son of Man and spoke in the name of the Son of Man. While he sometimes, as here, used the expression in the ordinary Aramaic sense of man, he often used it of himself as representing mankind: "For the Son of

Man has come to search for what was lost and to save it"
(Luke 19:10).

The Sabbath was one of the basic institutions of Judaism, and the Pharisees guarded it with the most intense
fervor. Originally instituted for the relief of the overbur-
dened laborer, Pharisaic refinements and definitions had
smothered its noble intention with petty detail. One must
not make a journey on the Sabbath. But how far was a
"journey"? They settled on a thousand yards as the maxi-
mum distance allowable. The rabbis specified thirty-nine
kinds of work that must not be done, and had of course to
indicate how much of any kind of activity constituted
work. A man might be given medical aid only if his life
was in danger.

So while Jesus in some important aspects of his work
was quite in line with the better class of Pharisees, at other
points he was not, and these incidents and conversations
were naturally causing the Pharisees of Capernaum, who
were recognized as the representative religious people
there, to be dissatisfied with him as a religious teacher, and
to find themselves differing sharply with him. But their
objections to him changed to open hostility when he cured
a man with a withered hand, in the synagogue on the
Sabbath day. He called the man to the front, and boldly
challenged the Pharisees before the congregation.

"Is it allowable," he asked, "to do people good on the
Sabbath, or to do them harm? To save life, or to kill?"
Then he said to the man,

"Hold out your hand!"

He held it out, and it was cured.

This dramatic rebuke of them and their position crystallized the Pharisaic attitude toward him into mortal enmity, and they got together with the Herodians, probably functionaries or agents of the court of Herod Antipas, the governor of Galilee, to secure his execution, as a breaker of the Sabbath, in accordance with Old Testament law.

News of this danger soon reached Jesus and his circle. There were many disciples of John there, and Jesus himself now had a good many partisans in Capernaum and in Galilee generally, so news of his danger was bound to reach him before long. It was not at all impossible that he would be done away with on some pretext or other, to satisfy the local Pharisees who had now become definitely his enemies. To execute him by stoning, for breaking the Law, might be impossible, but their relations with Herod's people could easily supply the means for their end. John himself had been picked up by Herod's people—just such Herodians—and was in prison, though his end was not far off.

The shadow of the cross already falls across the gospel story, though Jesus has been at work only a few weeks.

It was a very serious situation. Jesus has no mind to meet death needlessly, in an obscure corner of Galilee, before he has had any chance to lay his message before the Jewish people, and he and his disciples, the five or six closest ones, leave Capernaum for the "seashore." As Capernaum itself was on the shore of the lake, it is clear that if he withdrew from Capernaum it must have been for a distant part of the lake, probably the eastern side of it, where he could take counsel with his closest followers and plan his campaign. But crowds larger than ever now gather about him, our oldest account says not only from Galilee but from Judea and Jerusalem and Idumea and the other side of the Jordan—"Trans-Jordan"—and even from the neighborhood of Tyre and Sidon, away over on the Mediterranean. He has to have a boat at hand to get into when the multitude threaten to crush him in their frantic eagerness to reach him. His passion for helping the afflicted, the sick and demon-possessed, as they considered them, still controls him.

Escaping from the throngs of people, he led his disciples up the hillside, and summoned others whom he wished especially to see. Out of these he selected twelve, to form an inner circle of his followers and be his associates and messengers. This recalls what Isaiah had done, centuries before, when he encountered discouraging opposition, and began to devote himself to teaching an inner circle of disciples, to whom he might, as it were, seal the testimony and entrust it in hope of a better day to come. And Jesus now began to use a different method of instruction, resorting to parables, which without angering the pious might carry his great messages to his more thoughtful hearers.

The group of apostles, or messengers, began with the four fishermen he had probably known in John's camp meetings: Simon, whom he afterward called Peter, Andrew, James and John. The last two he nicknamed Boanerges, Aramaic for "sons of thunder." The others were Philip, Bartholomew, Matthew (probably another name for Levi), Thomas, James, son of Alpheus, Thaddeus (called Judas, son of James, in Luke 6:16), Simon the Zealot, and Judas Iscariot. The Zealots were a body of revolutionaries to which this second Simon belonged or had belonged.

That Isaiah and his tragic experience were in Jesus' mind in these early days of his work appears again soon after, when the disciples asked him about his use of parables, to which they evidently objected, and he told them the meaning of their close association with himself.

"To you," he said, "has been entrusted the secret of the reign of God. But to those outsiders everything is offered in figures, so that

" 'They may look and look and yet not see,
And listen and listen and yet not understand;
Lest possibly they should turn and be forgiven.' "

These were the bitter words which Isaiah used when his message was falling on deaf ears, and making no impression on his audiences. So not only in the choosing of an inner circle of disciples, to whom he might impart the secret of the reign of God, but also in his new method of speaking, half-veiling his meaning in this new parabolic form, he certainly had Isaiah's experience in mind, for he says so.

In a famous and dramatic passage, Isaiah showed the use and probably the purpose he intended for his band of disciples, when in a mood of disappointment, almost of desperation, he said,

"I will bind up my testimony, and seal my teaching in the heart of my disciples; then I will wait for the Lord, who is hiding his face from the house of Israel; I will set my hope on him" (Isaiah 8:16, 17). There can be no doubt that Jesus had this utterance of Isaiah in mind when, already threatened with death, he formed his own band of close disciples, and entrusted to them the secret of the reign of God. And it must not be forgotten that Isaiah is generally understood to have been put to death for his work, and that such success as Jesus' work achieved was in no small degree due to the measures he was now taking, for in taking it up and carrying it forward these disciples, most of them, played heroic parts. So we may think of Isaiah, his words and his measures and his fate, as being much in Jesus' mind in those crucial days in Galilee.

One of the disciples, it is true, was notoriously false to his Master; and even Peter failed him in the great moment. But none of the others rose to the commanding stature Peter afterward achieved, when he made good his title as the first of the apostles. It is, as we have seen, in every way probable that it was his memories of Jesus' work and teaching that after his death took form as the first written gospel, the Gospel of Mark, while to Matthew ancient tradition assigned the composition of the earliest, unwritten, oral gospel which was known and used by Paul and his generation, being in fact the only gospel they possessed. Yes, what Jesus called the secret of the reign of God was passing into faithful hands.

There can be little doubt that the twelve men whom

Jesus gathered about him on that mountainside across the lake received some vital instruction from him before they descended the mountain and took the boat back to Capernaum. For that is what they did; Jesus and his twelve followers returned home. His plans were made, and he began to see his course opening before him; and his flight from the plotting Pharisees was only a temporary retirement from the scene. If he can keep these men about him, and teach and train them, his work will go on, even if he is taken away.

It is at this point in the story that Luke has his brief account of the sermon we know so well in Matthew as the Sermon on the Mount, a sweeping statement of the kind of life the kingdom of God demanded of its members.

CHAPTER VI

Jesus' Preaching:
The Sermon on the Mount

"The reported sayings of Christ," said Professor White-head, "are not formularized thought. They are descriptions of direct insight. The ideas are in his mind as immediate pictures. . . . He sees intuitively the relations between good men and bad men. . . . He speaks in the lowest abstractions that language is capable of. . . . In the Sermon on the Mount, and in the Parables, there is no reasoning about the facts. They are seen with immeasurable innocence." . . .

It is a tragic fact that all that the gospels report of what Jesus said, in private and in public, he could have uttered in two hours. How little of his teaching has been preserved! Yet that little was so stirring, so moving and so penetrating that it is safe to say nobody else has influenced the world so much. But think of it! To be able to say in two hours enough to change the current of mankind!

The Gospel of Matthew in Chapters 5, 6 and 7 gathers a body of Jesus' sayings into a great sermon, famous beyond all other speeches ever made as the Sermon on the Mount.

It is one of the things that led Renan to say that the Gospel of Matthew was the most important book in the world. It is a tremendous formulation of the attitudes that were to prevail in the kingdom of heaven, and yet, though it set human relations on a new footing, it could all have been uttered in twenty minutes. Where else in all history was so much said in so short a time? It is the program of a new day in man's morals. This is how he is to act, in the new kingdom of heaven, the reign of God on earth, which Jesus was actually inaugurating.

The evangelist presents it in a most dramatic manner. Jesus' preaching in Galilee has been a great success. Crowds of people from other parts of Palestine—Decapolis and Judea, even Jerusalem and Trans-Jordan—follow him wherever he goes. And seeing this, he goes up on the mountain! What an extraordinary thing to do, for he can hardly hope the crowds can follow him there! Up on the mountain, he seats himself—a signal that he is about to teach, for the Jewish teacher sat, and his hearers stood. His disciples understand his action and gather about him to hear what he is going to say, and he opens his lips to teach them.

What is the meaning of this elaborate introduction, with its strange setting—on the mountain—and its almost pontifical climax: "he opened his lips to teach them"? Of course it means that what he is now about to say is of the utmost importance and value. For the reference to the mountain would recall at once to the Jewish mind another great religious teacher, who went up on the mountain—

and came down with the tables of the Law! What has the new teacher to compare with that great communication? The evangelist's confident answer is the Sermon on the Mount.

We do not ordinarily think of Jesus as a poet, but the Sermon on the Mount begins with a poem. For the Beatitudes are certainly a psalm. Think of how often this ecstatic use of "Blessed" appears in the poetry of the Old Testament! Blessed is the man . . . Blessed is the nation . . . Blessed is the people . . . Blessed are they . . . Blessed are you. . . . It is found a score of times in the poetry of Isaiah, the Proverbs, but especially of course the Psalms. Certainly, the Beatitudes are the Psalm of Jesus:

Blessed are those who feel their spiritual need,
     for the kingdom of heaven belongs to them!
Blessed are the mourners,
     for they will be consoled!
Blessed are the humble-minded,
     for they will possess the land!
Blessed are those who are hungry and thirsty for uprightness,
     for they will be satisfied!
Blessed are the merciful,
     for they will be shown mercy!
Blessed are the pure in heart,
     for they will see God!
Blessed are the peace-makers,
     for they will be called God's sons!
Blessed are those who have endured persecution for their
          uprightness,
     for the Kingdom of Heaven belongs to them!

Blessed are you when people abuse you, and persecute you,
  and falsely say everything bad of you, on my account!
Be glad and exult over it, for you will be richly rewarded in
  heaven,
    for that is the way they persecuted the prophets who went
    before you!

This vivid setting forth of the standards of happiness in
the new kingdom is, of course, basic to the presentation of
the ethics of the kingdom that follows. The ninefold
Beatitudes have no precise parallel in the Psalter, but there
is a sixfold sequence at the beginning of the Song of the
Three Children—the Benedicite—in the Apocrypha. This
striking beginning of the great sermon has also had a separate history of its own, as a beloved piece of Christian
liturgy, the Beatitudes. For Luke's set of four, followed by
four curses, in the old Hebrew manner, while powerfully
put in the second person, and in some ways of a more primitive sound than Matthew's, need not have been the only
instance of Jesus' employing this telling way of presenting
his religious ideals. Indeed, Matthew too employs the
direct form, Blessed are you, as the climax of the Beatitudes as he gives them. And obviously both series reflect
the later persecution experience of the early church (Luke
6:22, 23). So Matthew's may be thought of as an assem-
bling of such blessings, uttered at various times; the whole
sermon is probably built up from Matthew's sources into
its present proportions. As Walter Pater said, the genius
for liturgy was one of the chief endowments of the early

church. Yet neither in these Beatitudes, nor in the sermon is there anything that can be called a relaxation or abatement of Jesus' lofty ethics, anything that suggests any reduction of his own great ideals. These are not things the evangelists could have conjured up; they bear the stamp of Jesus' mind and spirit.

For while many of the Old Testament beatitudes are, to the religious mind, so obvious as to be almost trite, Jesus' beatitudes startle every age. The mourners, the humble-minded, the persecuted—how can they be called happy? For that is what the word means, and that is the way John Wesley translated it, two hundred years ago. Certainly they present an amazing picture of the Christian character, in nine immensely bold and telling strokes. It is not the self-satisfied people, who are proud and complacent about their religious achievements, not the gay, laughing people, not the proud, not the self-righteous, not the cruel, the impure, the belligerent, the persecuting, the abusive—why, those who are the victims of such people are more blessed than they are. This is the poem with which the sermon begins.

While the sermon is to some extent colored by the times when the Gospel of Matthew was written, it still brings us with amazing vividness into the very presence of Jesus. His followers are the salt of the earth, the light of the world. The great moral values of the Law are eternal; and high rank in the new kingdom of heaven awaits those who not only teach it but observe it, as the scribes and Pharisees do not. It is not only in overt act but even more in inner attitude that uprightness consists. Evil desire, willful divorce, needless oaths, retaliation, hatred of one's enemies, ostentatious praying, giving and fasting—these are wrong. We must trust the care of God, and not go after wealth. Uprightness and character that will please him are the only worthy goals for our efforts.

Jesus saw that religion could never be adequately set forth as a legislation to be obeyed. The Torah was a legal code, of crimes to be punished, not a moral standard, of ideals to be attained. What men needed was to be kept from anger and contempt, and calling each other vile names, against which the Torah had nothing to say. Adulterous wishes and frivolous divorces are morally wrong. It is not enough to avoid perjury; men must speak the truth. Over against the Torah, as Whitehead says, the life of Christ has the decisiveness of a supreme ideal.

Much is being said nowadays in praise of Pharisaism, and it had indeed had a noble beginning, in resistance to the compulsory assimilation to Hellenism that Antiochus the king of Syria had tried to force upon his subjects two centuries before. The Jewish Puritans of his day formed a body of Separatists, who would not conform to his demands or give up their distinctive national and religious habits of life. The triumph of their cause transformed their position from a desperately heroic situation to one of importance and privilege. They found themselves the custodians, as they thought, of the true religion of Israel, the core of which was for them the Law, the Torah, the five books of Moses. These they canonized and idolized, embellishing them with elaborate interpretations, which they held just as sacred as the Law itself. Judaism was thus made so elaborate that ordinary people, poor and struggling for existence, could not observe it, and passed out of the religious picture altogether. Judaism began to exclude even Jews, and hostility to the enemies of their culture sometimes passed into hate, as the last page of the Pharisaic II Maccabees so terribly shows. Nicanor, the Syrian general, is slain by Judas Maccabeus, who cuts off his head and his right arm, and takes them to Jerusalem in triumph, and there he cuts out Nicanor's tongue, and says he will cut it in pieces and feed it to the birds. This is what Jesus referred to when he said,

"You have heard that they were told, 'You must love your neighbor and hate your enemy.' But I tell you, love your enemies!"

Judaism, especially as the Pharisees developed it, was essentially a calculating religion. It was based on an agreement, to be observed by both parties. The Law told the Jews just what was expected of them, or so they thought, and the Pharisees and their rabbis had ironed out any possible uncertainties it might have left, so that one young man could say to Jesus,

"I have observed all these commandments ever since I was a child!" The Pharisee in the parable stood up and uttered this prayer to himself: "O God, I thank you that I am not like other men, greedy, dishonest, or adulterous, like that tax-collector. I fast two days in the week, I pay tithes on everything I get." He was the symbol of the complacent Jew, who felt that he had fulfilled the Law, and so done all God asked of him.

But to Jesus, what God asked was something very different. It was an attitude of such indefatigable kindness to one's fellow-men that even the harsh demand of their Roman masters for enforced personal service—carrying a Roman soldier's baggage for a mile for him, if demanded— is not to be refused, or even resented, but so cheerfully performed that a second mile of service is volunteered, out of sheer good will. They must indeed be perfect, like their heavenly Father. This carried his followers out of the realm of Jewish attitudes altogether. It went beyond the Golden Rule. It was, as Dr. Colwell puts it, no "measure for measure" morality.

When they pray, they must not resort to long strings of empty phrases, like the heathen. New light has been thrown on Jesus' meaning by the Isis Litany, probably contemporary with Jesus (the Oxyrhynchus papyrus of it is of the early second century), which recites a long series of titles given to Isis in different places, as well as the functions ascribed to her; the papyrus, though only a fragment apostrophizing the goddess, takes ten minutes to read aloud. Jesus offered his disciples a prayer of the utmost brevity and simplicity, which became and remains the most valued treasure of his followers everywhere. Yet its recital takes hardly more than half a minute.

But to paraphrase or summarize the Sermon on the Mount is futile. It is so crisply, forcibly put that any substitute falls far short of doing it justice. The gospels have long been recognized as the most effective form of religious literature ever devised, and their chief advantage lies in their abundant use of the sayings of Jesus, which are at once so winning and so searching. With a sure touch they probe the human heart, and offer the moral remedy in words of such vigor, originality and attractiveness that they are unforgettable. Many people say their religion is the Sermon on the Mount. Certainly it is the greatest statement of the ethics of the kingdom of heaven.

What Jesus had discerned was that the reign of God was not something to be postponed to some distant future, but a present reality to be entered into and personally realized; that God's great wealth of love and consideration was simply waiting to be accepted and adopted in men's hearts. He brought the reign of God, the kingdom of heaven, out of future fatalism into the present tense, and proposed that men should do something about it—one reason his religion not long afterward so strongly gripped the Western world. He also declared its program to be self-help and mutual help, each life to be a present, immediate channel for the love and compassion and mercy of God. All we now see of social co-operation in the world we owe to him. It is no accident that the least co-operative countries in the world today are atheistic.

It is hardly necessary to say that the amount of sheer insight, truth and indefatigable good will packed into the Sermon on the Mount is almost incalculable. It is a little gospel all by itself. It may seem only idealistic, but the modern world is coming to see that the remarkable thing about it is its sheer realism; nothing else will actually work.

The Sermon on the Mount *told* Jesus' hearers how to live in the kingdom of heaven; his own life of tireless usefulness *showed* them how to do it. He went about doing good. That this was the real sense the early church drew from his life is shown by the bold words of the Gospel of John, eighty years later: "Whoever believes in me will do such things as I do, and things greater yet, because I am going to the Father."

Through his sermons and parables he shows that "first-hand intuition into the nature of things" of which Whitehead speaks.

CHAPTER VII

Preaching and Conflict in Galilee

We must not in our comfort and security fail to note that it took no little courage for Jesus to return to Capernaum. The Pharisees might not indeed be able to get him put to death for breaking the Sabbath, but their mysterious combination with the Herodians was capable of any degree of violence. Herod's agents could easily do to him what they had only a few weeks before done to John, whose popularity had aroused the suspicions of Herod. He had imprisoned him, Josephus tells us (*Antiquities* xviii.5. 2), in the remote fortress of Machaerus, on the precipitous eastern shores of the Dead Sea. The Pharisees through their Herodian allies could easily bring about Jesus' imprisonment, at the very least. And in fact their hostility, as we shall see, pursued him the few remaining months of his life, though in the end it was not the Pharisees but the Sadducees who brought about his death.

As soon as Jesus with his enlarged following reached Capernaum, the crowds gathered as before, not so much to learn from his preaching as to witness his cures and exorcisms. He was so beset by them that he and his disciples had no chance even to have their meals. But there

86

were new figures among them now. His relatives had come over from Nazareth, a day's journey away, to stop him. James, his eldest brother, was doubtless at their head, that remarkable man who after Jesus' death became the leader of Jesus' Jewish followers and the head of the church in Jerusalem, the man who did so much to make the Christian movement a new variety of Pharisaism but found a great opponent in the apostle Paul.

Not only Nazareth but faraway Jerusalem has heard about Jesus, and scribes from there have appeared to declare that he is himself possessed by Beelzebub, and that is why he can drive out demons. Jesus deals with them first.

"How can Satan drive Satan out? If Satan has rebelled against himself, and become disunited, he cannot last long, but is nearing his end. No one can go into a strong man's house and carry off his property, unless he first binds the strong man! After that, he can plunder his house."

This was really a little parable, of the kind Jesus now proposes to employ. But after it, he speaks plainly, beginning with the expression he used to emphasize his words:

"I tell you, men will be forgiven for everything, for all their sins and all the abusive things they say. But whoever reviles the holy Spirit can never be forgiven, but is guilty of an unending sin!"

He felt himself possessed with the spirit of God and he would not tolerate any disparagement of that endowment.

Then came his mother and his brothers. Joseph was probably dead by this time; certainly the silence about him in the gospels would lead us to think so. But Jesus had four younger brothers, James, Joseph, Judah and Simon, living at Nazareth, and his sisters also lived there. Yet when he came back from the wilderness full of his new mission, he had not gone there, but had come right up to Capernaum, it would seem, to look up his old comrades of John's meetings. Evidently his brothers had not shared his great interest in John's work or joined the number of his disciples.

They found the house crowded with his hearers and sent word in to him to come out and talk to them; they were not inclined to join his audience in the house. But when he was told that his mother and his brothers were outside asking to see him, he answered,

"Who are my mother and my brothers?"

Then looking around at the people sitting about him he said,

"Here are my mother and my brothers! Whoever does the will of God is my brother and sister and mother!"

In this immensely striking way, he placed the ties formed in his religious fellowship above those of birth and family, and adopted his followers as his relatives. Jesus later gave classic expression to this attitude when he said (Matthew 10:37),

"No one who loves father or mother more than he loves me is worthy of me."

He now resumed his teaching on the lake shore. But such a crowd gathered that he was obliged to get into a boat and, putting out a little way from land, to speak from it to the throng gathered on the beach. And now he begins that new approach which he was to find so fruitful, and make so famous, that it has come to be actually identified with him; it was the parable. The parable is an application of fiction to moral instruction. Nathan in II Samuel 12 had used it, with the story of the poor man's ewe lamb, and Isaiah used it (Chapter 5) in the story of God's vineyard. The leading rabbis of Jesus' day also spoke in parables. But Jesus used parables so often and so effectively that many people to this day actually think he originated the parable, or monopolized it.

There was, to begin with, the immensely suggestive parable of the sower, such a warning to careless, casual listeners. It seemed to say to them, "Look out! Which kind of ground are you going to be?" It appealed at once to the familiar experiences and observation of his audiences, and entertained them as narratives generally entertain, but left in thoughtful and inquiring minds a deep religious suggestion. This was only one of the many stories he told the crowd there on the lake shore, not drawing any morals but leaving the explanation to the listeners themselves. The parable had all the attraction of a puzzle or a problem. What did he mean by it? they would inevitably ask themselves. He quickened their interest and curiosity by adding,

"Let him who has ears be sure to listen!"

There was more in the story, he wanted them to see, than met the eye, as we say; it called for close attention and reflection.

In another parable, he told the people by the lake of a man who sows his seed, and then turns to other things, while the seed comes up, and the crop ripens. Only when the harvesttime comes does he get out his sickle and begin to reap. We must have similar patience about the purposes of God. And as for the apparent insignificance of our efforts, look at the tiny mustard seed, that grows into something as large as a tree; why, the wild birds come and roost under its protection.

Only in such parables—the Tares, or weeds, the Seed Growing by Itself, the Hoard, the Pearl, the Fish Net— did Jesus now preach to the people of Galilee. But he explained much of what he said in private to his disciples. The seed was the word that he preached. The secret that he had told them about the reign of God was secret only that it might sometime be disclosed.

"Do people get out a lamp," he asked, "and then put it under the peck measure, or under the bed, instead of putting it up where it belongs?" The ancient lamp (the ancients did not use candles) was a little clay or metal affair, three or four inches across and an inch high, filled with oil, with a little wick, which to be of any use had to be put on a stand thirty or forty inches high, so that it could cast its feeble rays about the room. To push it under the bed, or cover it with a peck measure would make it useless; nobody would do such a thing, with a lamp anyway. But he might do something just as foolish with his powers and gifts, or even his life. A time would come when the lamp would be set up to give its full light.

They must give full measures; if they do, they will receive full measures, and even more will be added, a paradoxical observation, yet profoundly true.

When his explanations to his disciples were concluded, he told them to cross the lake to the other side. The lake is only eight miles across but, set as it is in the mountains, it is liable to sudden storms. When they were well on their way across, one of these now swept down upon it. Jesus was lying in the stern, asleep on a cushion, when they woke him with a reproach:

"Master, does it make no difference to you that we are sinking?"

But he calmed their fears, and bade the waves subside. The wind went down, and sea was calm again. He said to them,

"Why are you afraid? Have you still no faith?"

He kept up their courage until the danger was over—always, of course, the religious approach to peril. God does not excuse us from it, but he will give us the courage to face it.

When I visited the Sea of Galilee in my student days, fifty years ago, the boats in use were sailboats some twenty-two feet long and eight feet wide, which the five native boatmen rowed when the wind failed. There were four of us in addition to the boatmen, and we were not crowded. I suppose the boats in use on the lake in Jesus' day were much the same, and it must have been in such a boat that Jesus and his disciples after the storm landed on the other side of the lake at Gerasa, probably the modern Kersa, on the eastern shore, at the widest point of the lake, directly opposite Magdala. Mark cannot mean the town of Gerasa, or Jerash, down in the Decapolis, some thirty-five miles in a straight line from the lake. Matthew speaks of the place as Gadara, another Decapolis town, six miles southeast of the lake, across the river Yarmuk.

As they landed, there met them from among the tombs a poor demoniac, who came running up and bowed low to Jesus. Jesus immediately uttered his characteristic words of exorcism:

"You foul spirit, come out of him!"

"What do you want of me?" screamed the poor fellow. "In God's name I implore you not to torture me!"

Jesus calmed him with a question.

"What is your name?"

"My name is Legion!" cried the man, "for there are many of us!" This was clearly the man's own conviction of his emotional instability; he felt himself to be in the control of a multiple personality. He could only beg Jesus to send all the hordes of demons that he felt possessed him into a great drove of pigs that were feeding on the neighboring headland. Jesus humored him, and the man's cries and movements so frightened the animals that they rushed in panic over the edge of the cliff into the lake.

The swineherds hurried off in dismay to tell the news in the town and the country round, and the people came streaming out to see what had happened. They found the demoniac sitting quietly with his clothes on and in his right mind, a great contrast to his former condition when they had felt obliged to chain him up, and even that did not restrain him. But they were heathen, for Jews could not keep pigs, and were more concerned with the loss of their pigs than with the recovery of the demoniac. So they begged Jesus to leave their district.

Only the poor demoniac hated to see him go, and begged to be allowed to go with him. But Jesus would not permit this.

"Go home to your own people," said he, "and tell them all the Lord has done for you, and how he took pity on you." So the man went off, telling all over Decapolis—the country of the Ten Towns—what Jesus had done for him.

Jesus and his disciples now set sail for the western shore of the lake, which at this point was eight miles across; they were probably all with him on this tour of the lake, for he had just appointed them to be his companions. One such boat as I found on the lake fifty years ago would have held them all, but Mark says that other boats were with Jesus when he set out to cross the lake to Gerasa. Just where he landed on the western side is not stated. He proved to be on his way to Nazareth, and Tiberias, well down the west shore, would seem the natural point to make. But Tiberias was built on the site of a graveyard, and considered by the Jews unclean; the town is never mentioned in the New Testament. From Magdala a few miles north of Tiberias, and some six miles south of Capernaum, a well-known road led to Nazareth, a day's journey to the southwest.

When Jesus landed he was met by the usual crowds, but this might by now have happened anywhere along the west shore.

As Jesus stood there, facing the crowd that gathered, the leader of the local synagogue approached him and threw himself at his feet.

"My little daughter," he said, "is at the point of death. Come, lay your hands on her so that she may get well and live!"

Jesus immediately set off with him to his house, followed by the crowd which had already gathered about him. As they went a woman with a chronic hemorrhage came close to him as he passed and touched his cloak, convinced that if she could only touch his clothes she would get well. As she touched it, she felt relief and the conviction that she was cured.

Jesus noticed the incident, and stopped, to ask who had touched him. The disciples protested that with the crowd around him it was unreasonable to ask such a question. But the woman came forward to tell him what she had done and what she felt had happened to her, and he replied,

"My daughter, it is your faith that has cured you. Go in peace, and be free from your disease."

Again, as so often, he pointed them to God as the source of all their relief and blessing. The gospels do not give us this woman's name, but a woman of Magdala named Mary later proved one of Jesus' most devoted followers, following him even to his crucifixion and death.

But even as he spoke, people came from the synagogue leader's house to report that his daughter was dead, and that it was of no use to trouble the Master any further.

Jesus, however, disregarded them, and told the synagogue leader not to be afraid or lose his faith. Then he took Peter, James and John and leaving the others behind he hurried to the house. There the lamentation for the dead had already begun, they were so sure the child was gone. But Jesus said to them,

"What is the meaning of all this confusion and crying? The child is not dead, she is asleep."

Then turning the wailers out, he took his three disciples and the child's parents and went to her bedside, grasped her hand and said to her in Aramaic,

"Little girl, get up!"

To their utter amazement the child obeyed, got to her feet and walked. He forbade them to tell of it, but told them to give her something to eat.

But the furor these two cures must have produced, a form of popularity he had already found unfavorable to his great religious message, hastened his departure from the town, and he set off with his band of disciples for Nazareth, a walk of some seven or eight hours. The road from Magdala or any of the principal west-shore towns led through the mountains then very much as it does now, through Hattin, Lubieh, Khan et-Tujjar and Kefr Kenna to Nazareth, which was pleasantly situated on the northern slope of a basin of hills, facing toward the south. A fine spring, now known as the Virgin's Well, gave the town its water supply, and from the hilltop a short walk above the town and 1600 feet above the sea, there was, as there is today, a magnificent view. The traveler can still see Mount Carmel, to the west, with the Bay of Acre above it; to the northeast, Mount Hermon, snow capped; to the east-northeast, the far blue line of the Jaulan; to the east-southeast, Mount Tabor, close at hand, with the hills of Gilead behind it; to the south, Little Hermon, and to the right of it the great plain of Esdraelon, with the hills of Samaria—"Mount Ephraim"—behind. One seems to see the whole land, except Judea, at a single glance, and all of it strangely close at hand. So at least I saw it, from the dome of a dilapidated *wely*, or sheikh's tomb. And one can safely think of Jesus as having often seen it, in his boyhood, youth and manhood, in the thirty years he spent at Nazareth.

Nazareth is not mentioned in the Old Testament, or in the Talmud. It was not at all a famous or historic town. The remark of Nathanael in John 1:46, "Can anything good come from Nazareth?" probably means no more than this: Jewish feeling expected good and great men to come only from places previously distinguished in their long religious history, and Nazareth was not such a place.

One wonders whether Jesus now resumed relations with his family. One purpose of his visit must certainly have been to satisfy his own people of the worth of his message and the reality of his mission. When the Sabbath came, he appeared in the synagogue, as he had so often done, and began to teach.

Luke says that there was given him the roll of the prophet Isaiah, and that he unrolled it and found the place where it says

"The spirit of the Lord is upon me,
　For he has consecrated me to preach the good news
　　to the poor,
　He has sent me to announce to the prisoners their
　　release, and to the blind the recovery of their sight,
　To set the down-trodden at liberty,
　To proclaim the year of the Lord's favor!"

Then he rolled up the roll, and gave it back to the attendant, and sat down to teach. The eyes of everyone in the synagogue, Luke goes on, were fixed upon him. And he began by saying to them,

"This passage of scripture has been fulfilled, here in your hearing today!"

This was the nearest thing to an assertion of his Messianic mission that he had yet made, in public, as far as our earliest records, Mark, Matthew and Luke show. Certainly he was here identifying himself with God's Suffering Servant, of the later chapters of Isaiah.

Not long ago, on February 19, 1948, a young American scholar, Dr. John C. Trever, discovered in Jerusalem a scroll of Isaiah twenty-four feet in length, written in the second century before Christ, and so actually old enough to have been used by Jesus in the synagogue in Nazareth, in A.D. 29. We cannot, of course, for a moment claim that this is so, but it was doubtless just such a scroll of Isaiah as this one, found so lately in a cave high above the Dead Sea, that Jesus received from the attendant, found the place in (61:1, 2), read the Hebrew lesson from, translating it into Aramaic as he read, and then handed back to the synagogue attendant. Certainly to the student of the life of Jesus no archaeological discovery could be more welcome and moving.

This newly discovered scroll of Isaiah enables us to reconstruct just what must have happened before that congregation in Nazareth. Only one side of it was written on; the back was left blank. The Isaiah scroll was not mounted on sticks or rollers, as rolls of the Law now are, but was rolled up as one roll with the beginning on the outside, as traces of the ancient cover show. Jesus probably laid it on a desk or lectern, since he would read it standing. The soil and stain along the middle of the back of the Dead Sea scroll are the evident result of much handling in rolling and unrolling the scroll, to find a given passage. Jesus would thus have to unroll twenty-one feet of the leather scroll, probably rolling it up with his right hand as he unrolled with his left, to reach the forty-ninth column, where the lesson he wished to read, from the beginning of our Chapter 61, is found. But in this scroll, and in all such scrolls of that day, there were no chapter numbers, only occasional paragraphs, and one would have to know his way about the book of Isaiah extremely well to be able to find it.

As Luke tells the story, the first reaction of the congregation was one of astonishment and satisfaction; they were proud of their townsman:

"Isn't he Joseph's son?" they whispered to one another. But others said,

"Where did he get all this?"

"How does he come to have such wisdom?"

"How are such marvelous things done through him?"

"Isn't he the carpenter, Mary's son, and the brother of James, Joseph, Judah and Simon? And aren't his sisters living here among us?"

And when he went on to tell them that no prophet was ever welcome in his own country, and remind them that Elijah and Elisha did their greatest wonders outside of Israel, they were greatly incensed and got up and hurried him rudely out and up the hillside he knew so well to the top of the Jebel-es-Sikh, to throw him over the precipice. But with his awe-inspiring mien, he strode through the midst of them and was gone.

Jesus was surprised at the failure of the people of Nazareth to show any faith in him, but he continued on his way, teaching among the villages.

CHAPTER VIII

Sending Out the Twelve

For some weeks now Jesus has had the twelve disciples with him as he moves about Galilee and to and fro across the lake. The time he spent in preaching to the people, in their synagogues or out of doors on the seashore (the ancient world was used to street preaching—it was a practice of the Stoics) was much less however than that he devoted to instructing these more intimate followers of his, to whom he was imparting what he called the secret of the reign of God, that conception of religion which Pharisaic legalists would not permit him to proclaim to the people generally. Jesus was not afraid of them, but he had no mind to be cut off with his work undone, and he did not underestimate their influence with the authorities of Galilee. He had learned the lesson of the fate of John, for whom he entertained the highest admiration and regard. And it was Herod Antipas, the governor of Galilee, who had arrested John, and shut him up in prison, and had probably already put him to death.

But his own time might be all too short, and he moved rapidly. In the course of the few weeks of this intimate schooling, he told them such things as his extraordinary

experience at his baptism, and gave them an account of
his temptation experiences so immensely dramatic that no
one else could possibly have expressed it. The style of Jesus
was in fact one of amazing imagination and vigor. It has
been characterized as "gigantesque"—and this is no exaggeration. One explorer of the gospels after another has felt
this in Mark particularly. The Gospel of Mark consists for
the most part of a series of pictures or incidents, situations
into which Jesus comes, and which he remedies, by doing
something or saying something utterly unusual. And his
remarks on these occasions flash forth like a bright sword,
against the background of the evangelist's narrative—vivid,
trenchant and revealing. There is an entire absence of the
commonplace from his remarks and his discourses.
Certainly the men who wrote the gospels were quite incapable of having originated them. Even the influence of
the Old Testament prophets and Psalmists on them is rel-
atively slight.

And yet as he went about the villages of populous
Galilee it was what he did rather than what he said that
won him fame. Wherever he went he did people good.
It is the Gospel of Mark that makes this most apparent.
He was ever the Doer; the Man of Action. In fact, it
was an act of his that brought about his death, for it was
really his clearing the temple of its abuses that sealed his
fate in Jerusalem a few months later.

It is a striking fact that so many of the doings that the
early evangelists recorded about him so much resemble
the kind of thing the books of Kings relate of Elijah and

Elisha, and we must conclude that they felt his whole activity was reminiscent of theirs. The selective memory of the early church seized upon everything in Jesus' life and work that had any kind of parallel in the wonders done by those great prophets, so deeply had Malachi's idea of a new Elijah as the forerunner of the day of the Lord possessed them.

As we have seen, Isaiah's purpose in confiding his message to his disciples was to preserve it in their minds so that when he was taken away it might yet survive. But Jesus has a more immediate object. He proposes to train his disciples and then send them out over the land to carry his message everywhere. But he first gives them some detailed instructions as to their equipment and procedure.

While Mark speaks briefly of this extraordinary forward step on Jesus' part, Matthew reports it in considerable detail. We may think of Jesus as returned to Capernaum, which seems to have been his headquarters. He sends the disciples, who are now to be indeed apostles—"messengers" —to carry his message to the Jewish people. They are to go out in pairs, and Matthew seems to give the actual pairs as they were constituted. The leaders are Simon and Andrew, Jesus' very first disciples. Then come those other brothers James and John; then Philip and Bartholomew; Thomas and Matthew, the tax collector; James the son of Alpheus, and Thaddeus; Simon the Zealot and Judas Iscariot, who afterward betrayed him.

They were to do good to those who were in need, as he had done. They had seen what an overwhelming sense of the love and mercy of God welled up within him and possessed him. The reign of God meant to him the spread of this attitude to all mankind. They were not to accept any payment at all for what they did, nor take any baggage, not even a change of clothes or shoes. They were to take no money, but seek and accept the hospitality of their hearers and, as long as they stayed in a place, not to move from the house that first received them; if no one would take them in, they were to shake off the dust of their feet as a warning to them.

Matthew amplifies these instructions with lessons that reflect the experience of Christian missionaries in the next fifty years. He undertook to bring them up to date, to serve the missionary needs of his day. The twelve were not to work among the heathen or the Samaritans, but to confine their efforts to "the lost sheep of Israel's house."

The twelve went out over Galilee, calling on the people to repent, in recognition of the reign of God. They carried on Jesus' ministry of helping the afflicted. Such a campaign must have created a decided sensation among the people, and it is not strange that word of it reached Antipas himself; he doubtless had his listening posts throughout the land, and Mark declares that he had an uneasy feeling that his old enemy John must have risen from the dead, and returned to haunt him.

On the completion of their preaching tour, the twelve returned to Jesus, to report and recruit. He was probably at Capernaum, and it would seem that they must have had a fairly definite time set for the completion of their mission. But at Peter's house in Capernaum, people are constantly coming and going, and Jesus at once proposes that they go away to some quiet place, and rest a little while. So they once more get into Peter's boat and set out for some secluded place, across the lake.

The eager crowds at headquarters were not to be so easily escaped, however, and, realizing their purpose, hurried around the shore of the lake to anticipate them. Crowds from the neighboring towns swelled their numbers, so that when their boat reached land, they found a great throng of people waiting for them.

Jesus was not annoyed or disconcerted by it, however. On the contrary, his heart was touched at the sight of them; he looked upon them as sheep that had no shepherd, and he plunged at once into the task of teaching them his great message of religion as an inner life, of repentance and acceptance of God's love and forgiveness.

He preached so long that the disciples came to ask him to send the people away to the farms and villages around, to get some food, for they were all far from their homes, and night was coming on.

But he answered,

"Give them food yourselves!"

They said to him,

"Can we go and buy forty dollars' worth of bread, and give it to them to eat?"

Of course the sum they mentioned had a purchasing power five times as great as it would have today. But he said to them,

"How many loaves have you? Go and see."

They looked, and told him,

"Five, and two fish."

He at once directed them all to sit down on the fresh grass. They threw themselves down in groups, by hundreds and fifties. Then he took the five loaves and the two fish, and looked up to heaven and blessed the loaves, and broke them in pieces, and gave them to the disciples to pass to the people. He also divided the two fish among them all. And they all ate, and had enough.

Jesus' simple example of sharing all he and his disciples had with their guests must have moved those Galileans as it moves us still. They could not do less than he had done. They followed his example. The story is an evidence of his power over their hearts, a power that has been exerted millions of times, and is exerted still. After all, it is his great example that has moved the world.

Generously distributed, there was plenty for them all. There was more than enough, for they later gathered up twelve baskets of pieces of bread and fish, left by the five thousand present. The feeding of the five thousand was a sermon in action. He taught them by example, on a grand scale, and they caught the spirit of his message of mutual concern and helpfulness.

Jesus had a tremendous personal attractiveness that made men want to follow him and do as he did. He did not have to bully or abuse them. He simply showed them the way, and they gladly took it. This has been his way ever since. He has made goodness and generosity attractive. He was the kind of man who could lead small groups, two or three, or twelve, and he was the kind of man who could lead thousands.

Jesus directed the disciples to take the boat and cross to the other side of the lake, toward Bethsaida, while he would dismiss the crowd. When he had done so, he went up on the hillside to pray, and in the evening the boat was out in the lake on its way, and he alone on the shore. He evidently meant to follow around the shore and rejoin them, as he did, for the wind was against them and their progress had been slow. Toward morning, excited and alarmed, they saw his ghostlike figure approaching them, as though walking on the sea, and thinking it was a ghost, they screamed with fear.

The first disciples and evangelists, we must remember, like almost everybody in their day, found it easy to believe in demons, ghosts, phantoms, and kindred marvels; it was their way of explaining what they did not understand. Like Antipas, they expected that sort of thing. We too have some popular "explanations" of what we do not understand, which the future may deem just as irrational.

Jesus immediately calmed their fears.

"Take courage," he said to them. "It is I. Don't be afraid," and got into the boat. The wind subsided; the storms on the lake are notoriously brief and violent. But the disciples were beside themselves with amazement and relief. He had planned to meet them toward Bethsaida, a mile or more east of the mouth of the Jordan, and now they set out for Capernaum and home. They landed at

Gennesaret, the fertile plain adjacent to Capernaum, and were at once again involved in all the usual crowds and excitement Jesus' appearance occasioned. People hurried over the countryside to report his return. The sick were brought in on their mats for his attention, wherever they heard he was, and laid in the market places where he was likely to pass, so that they might just touch the tassel of his robe.

CHAPTER IX

Jesus and John the Baptist

The few months of Jesus' active ministry are strangely interwoven with the work and fate of John the Baptist. It was the fame of John's preaching that had drawn Jesus from his carpenter's bench at Nazareth down to the Jordan thickets where John, a wilderness prophet whose clothes and ways made people think of Elijah, was thundering repentance and a mightier one to come in judgment after him. He found John all he had anticipated and more. He said afterward to his own disciples,

"I tell you, among men born of women no one has ever appeared, greater than John the Baptist. And yet," he went on, "those of little importance in the kingdom of God are greater than he." He felt that the light he could give his followers raised them above even John.

He had made the greatest friends of his life there in John's camp meetings by the Jordan—the men who afterward became his own first disciples and then the inner circle within the chosen band of the twelve.

He had found his own message and mission at his baptism, and in the succeeding weeks of moral struggle in the wilderness. The initial impulse to begin to preach came to him when on returning to the scene of John's meetings, he had found them gone, and John himself, by the orders of Antipas, hurried off to prison. The withdrawal of John from the scene cleared the way for Jesus to begin to preach, and he set out at once for Galilee, to find his old friends of John's fellowship, with his message of repentance and welcome for the good news of the reign of God now dawning upon the world.

Once when Jesus had been praying, his disciples said to him,

"Master, teach us to pray, as John taught his disciples."

That John had taught his disciples how to pray seems to have been the occasion for Jesus' doing so for his. Luke places this incident in the course of Jesus' last journey, through Trans-Jordan to Jerusalem, while Matthew incorporates it into the collection of Jesus' sayings on the way to live in the kingdom of heaven which we call the Sermon on the Mount. Matthew's form of it is somewhat longer and more liturgical than Luke's, which is without "thy will be done," and "deliver us from evil." But in use the prayer tended to be filled out into slightly fuller proportions, as the liturgical addition of the beautiful doxology, drawn from David's prayer in I Chronicles 29:11, 12, which we all use in worship, clearly shows. The origin of the prayer is probably just what Luke describes, and Jesus himself is very likely to have used it in a variety of forms. He probably intended it more as an example of what prayer should be than as a fixed and exclusive form of prayer.

John evidently felt that the current Pharisaic forms of prayer were not responsive to the deepest needs and aspirations of the religious heart. Jesus answered them with what we know as the Lord's Prayer, a prayer so simple and yet so searching that the mere utterance of it, in sincerity and understanding, calms and purifies and fortifies.

A touching glimpse of John's perplexities and hopes in the midst of his imprisonment was brought to Jesus by some of John's disciples, whom he sent to ask Jesus the great question: Was he indeed the long-expected one who was to come? John had heard through his disciples of Jesus' preaching and of his cures, and was naturally eager to know whether here was already the fulfiller of his own prediction of the one mightier than himself, for whom he had been so vigorously preparing the way; the one whom Malachi had prophesied so long ago.

Jesus' answer is of the utmost interest, for it bears decisively on the vital question of his own conception of his role and mission. He said to them,

"Go and report to John what you hear and see! The blind are regaining their sight and the lame can walk, the lepers are being cured and the deaf can hear, the dead are being raised and good news is being preached to the poor. And blessed is the man who finds nothing that repels him in me!"

He was quoting the great oracle of Isaiah 61:1, which Luke records Jesus read in the synagogue at Nazareth, as fulfilled in his work, and thus identifying himself not with the Jewish Messiah of ordinary expectation but with the

Suffering Servant of the Lord, of whom this part of Isaiah has so much to say. If he is to accept the great role of Messiah, that is the kind of Messiah he is to be.

When John's disciples were gone, Jesus went on to speak to his own followers about John. With his inimitable rhetoric he probed their motives and anticipations when months before they had flocked out to the wilderness to see John the Baptist. What did they expect to find? A weather vane? A courtier? It was a prophet that drew them out there, and more than a prophet! No other than the new Elijah, foretold in Malachi, sent to prepare the way.

"But to what," he went on, "can I compare this present age? It is like children sitting about in the bazaars, and calling out to their playmates,

" 'We have played the flute for you and you would
    not dance;
  We have wailed and you would not beat your
    breasts!'

For when John came, he neither ate nor drank, and people said, 'He has a demon!' Now that the Son of Man has come, he does eat and drink, and people say, 'Look at him! A glutton and a drinker, the companion of tax collectors and irreligious people!' And yet Wisdom is vindicated by her actions!"

It is plain that Jesus feels that he is carrying out the role of the Suffering Servant of Isaiah's prophecy, not at all the traditional Jewish view of the Messiah.

It was Herod Antipas who imprisoned John, evidently

snatching him away from the very midst of his great work of preaching on the lower Jordan, and after keeping him shut up in his castle of Machaerus, away on the eastern shores of the Dead Sea, put him to death, either there or in Tiberias. Josephus explains the action of Antipas as due to his fears that John might possibly stir up the people to revolt (*Antiquities* xviii.5. 2). But Mark had a much more intimate and personal explanation of John's death.

John had aroused the anger of Antipas when in his denunciation of the evils of the day he had pointed to the action of Antipas in putting away his lawful wife, the daughter of King Aretas of Arabia, and marrying Herodias, the wife of his half-brother Philip, whom he had seen in Rome and become infatuated with, and persuaded to leave her husband. This slight to the Arabian princess had led to a state of war with Aretas, which continued for some years. John had declared it was unlawful for Antipas to take his brother's wife. Even in prison Mark says that Herodias wanted him put to death for this, but that Antipas stood in awe of John and occasionally listened to what he had to say, though he found it very disturbing.

Herodias found her opportunity when in his birthday revels Antipas was entertaining his officers and courtiers, probably at his palace in Tiberias, which he had rebuilt in some splendor. In the course of this celebration, Herodias' daughter came in and with entire disregard of her rank gave a dance before the governor and his friends that so delighted him that he offered to give her anything she wanted. After going out to consult her mother, she came back to the banquet hall and said to the governor,

"I want you right away to give me John the Baptist's head on a platter!"

This horrible request sobered Antipas, but with all his boon companions about him he had not the courage to refuse, and he gave her what she asked. John was evidently at this time in prison at Antipas' capital, Tiberias. This daughter of Herodias is usually supposed to be the Salome who was, or became, the wife of Philip, the governor of the district northeast of the Sea of Galilee. When Philip died, five years later (A.D. 34), his domain was given to Herodias' brother Agrippa I. When in A.D. 36 Aretas destroyed the army of Antipas, Josephus says some of the Jews thought it was a punishment for Antipas' putting John to death.

A year later, after Philip's death, the willful Herodias again proved her husband's evil genius. The emperor Gaius on his accession in A.D. 37 gave what had been Philip's territory to Herodias' brother Agrippa I, with the title of king, something Antipas had never had officially, although the Gospel of Mark speaks of him as king. Herodias prevailed upon Antipas to visit Rome and ask a similar title for himself, but the new emperor exiled him to Lugdunum, the modern Lyons, instead, and Herodias decided to go with him.

CHAPTER X

The Second Clash with the Pharisees and the Retreat to the Sea

It is a striking fact that in crossing to the less populated east shore of the lake Jesus escaped from his Pharisaic critics, while his public, the plain people, followed him and heard him. But when he came back to the town, the Pharisees renewed their attack. They had been reinforced by some scribes, or legal experts, from Jerusalem, and noticed that some of his disciples ate their food without first giving their hands a ceremonial washing to purify them. Modern Jewish scholars declare that the Pharisees did not themselves demand this until many years after the time of Jesus, but as the Jews did not themselves record such matters or anything else in the first century, and in the nature of the case the practice grew up before it found a place in their rabbinic literature, it is unnecessary to try to correct Mark here. The truth is, the first gospels are our best and almost our only contemporary records of first-century Jewish practice in Palestine.

It must be remembered that the Palestine Jews of Jesus' day, in their abject devotion to the written Law of their religion, Genesis to Deuteronomy, purposely refrained from writing anything about religion, preferring to commit any worth-while decisions by their rabbis to memory and hand them down in that way. This was "the tradition of the elders," so often referred to in the gospels. Paul in his Pharisaic period had been fanatically devoted to what the forefathers had "handed down." In fact the Book of Enoch (from the first century before Christ), Chapter 69, expressly says that it was one of the fallen angels, Penemue, that taught men to write, "and thereby many have sinned from eternity to eternity and until this day. For men were not created for such a purpose, to give confirmation to their good faith with pen and ink"—69:9, 10. No wonder, in such an atmosphere, the decisions of the rabbis went for generations unwritten, and we may well wonder whether all of them were ever finally recorded. That is, the picture given in the late Mishnaic codification, about A.D. 200, may be expected to be far from complete, and its silence on a subject can hardly be treated as decisive evidence, over against a written record from the first century.

It is also noteworthy that in Luke's great account of the final journey through Trans-Jordan, this same practice comes up again, in a different district, and from a different source, unknown to Mark and itself unacquainted with Mark—a double attestation of the practice as in vogue on both sides of the Jordan, and in the south as well as the north. In the incident in Trans-Jordan, Luke 11:38, a Pharisee has invited Jesus to take lunch with him at his house, and observes that Jesus does not wash before eating. Jesus sees his surprise, and says to him,

"You Pharisees clean the outside of cups and dishes, but inside you are full of greed and wickedness. You fools! Did not the creator of the outside make the inside too? But give your inmost life as charity, and you will immediately find everything clean!"

A quarter-century ago it was argued by critics of the Gospel of Mark that Jewish records of first-century Jewish usage say nothing about the obligation of the ordinary Jew to wash his hands before his meals, though of course in the second century they have a great deal to say about it. But there are no contemporary Jewish records of the first century on this or any other subjects, as pointed out earlier.

But thus early in his ministry in Galilee, the Pharisees noticed that Jesus' disciples did not wash their hands in the approved ceremonious manner before eating, and they asked him to explain this disregard of the rules that had been handed down by tradition. Unlike the Sadducees, they regarded these decisions handed down by word of mouth as binding upon everybody.

Isaiah's great rebuke of his auditors came to his mind (how well he knew Isaiah!) and he answered them with the utmost vigor.

"It was about you hypocrites that Isaiah prophesied so finely when he said,

" 'This people honor me with their lips,
    Yet their hearts are far away from me.
    But their worship of me is all in vain,
    For the lessons they teach are but human precepts.'

"You give up what God has commanded, and hold fast to what men have handed down."

He went on to illustrate this attitude of theirs with a striking instance, ironically praising their skill in defeating the plain meaning of the Law by the technicalities of their tradition. The Law said a man must honor his parents, meaning of course among other things that he must support them if they needed it. But the rabbis had made a rule that if a man declared his property "Korban," that is, devoted to God, his parents could make no claim on him for their support. So while they loudly proclaimed their devotion to the Law, under the cloak of rabbinical de-·cisions they coolly evaded its most humane provisions.

He turned from them to the people, who were always at his heels, and gave *his* decision.

"Listen to me, all of you, and understand this: Nothing that goes into a man from outside can pollute him. It is what comes out of a man that pollutes him!"

In this utterance Jesus broke not simply with the regulations of the rabbis handed down among the Pharisees, but with the Mosaic Law itself, which in Leviticus, Chapter 11, gave long lists of birds, animals and insects which a Jew must not eat.

This is perhaps the most unequivocal instance in which Jesus definitely set aside not just the traditions of the rabbis, but the express provisions of the Jewish Law. And these were rules not simply for the priesthood but for all the Jewish people. Jesus afterward pointed out to what lengths a Pharisee would go to avoid swallowing a gnat if he saw one in what he was about to drink; why, he would go and strain the whole cupful, for fear of the religious defilement he would incur if he swallowed it. Yet the same man would have no such scruples about the far more important demands of the moral law.

No wonder the disciples, as soon as he had left the crowd and come home, asked him what he meant by such a sweeping statement. They could not believe their ears. The food regulations of Judaism had been one of its main safeguards against that assimilation to surrounding peoples which Judaism had been fighting so long and so desperately, and is fighting still.

The modern orthodox Judaism which preserves so much of first-century Pharisaic procedure confirms the central point of Jesus' criticism. A rare-book dealer of my acquaintance was recently entertained by another book expert in his old Jewish home in Philadelphia. He was asked what he would like for breakfast and unthinkingly mentioned bacon. "No bacon in this house!" his host cried out. "This house has been kosher for a hundred years." Jesus declared that it is not what goes into a man's mouth that defiles him, it is what comes out of his heart. And not only the grosser crimes, but the evil attitudes, greed, malice, deceit, indecency, envy, arrogance—all these come from within the man's heart, and they are the things that pollute him.

This was a clarion call to return to the basic elements of morals and religion. And it created such a state of tension with his adversaries in Capernaum that Jesus left there and once more passed out of the territory of Antipas, this time to the shores of the Mediterranean, and the region of Tyre and Sidon. A Roman road ran directly from near Capernaum north-northwest to Tyre, perhaps thirty-five miles away in a straight line. The road ran, and still runs, by Chorazin, Safed and Giscala to Tyre, certainly two or three days' journey on foot, as Jesus and the twelve traveled. Phoenicia had been made part of the province of Syria, so that there Jesus was quite out of the dominion of Antipas and the Herodian partisans of the Pharisees. With Jesus' determined policy of confining his work to his own people, this must have been intentional on his part, and designed to avoid a violent and probably perilous clash with his enemies in Galilee, of whose power to destroy, the recent fate of John had just given terrible proof. If Antipas could be instigated against him, anything might happen.

The seriousness with which Jesus himself viewed his situation is shown by the fact that he wanted nobody to know of his presence in the vicinity of Tyre. But as usually happened, this proved impossible, and a Greek woman of the province came to him to beg him to drive a demon out of her daughter. He answered her with startling brusqueness:

"Let the children first eat all they want, for it is not right to take the children's bread and throw it to the dogs."

He meant that his work must be for his own people. But she was too much in earnest to be hurt by his language, or perhaps something in his manner told her this was not really his own attitude, for she answered,

"True, sir! and still, the dogs under the table eat what the children leave!"

He felt the woman's earnestness and the real depth of her concern. This was no shallow request. He said to her,

"If you can say that, go home! The demon has left your daughter!"

He went on from Tyre up the coast as far as Sidon, and then eastward, still in Syrian territory, through Dan to Caesarea Philippi, the city rebuilt by Herod Philip and named in honor of Augustus Caesar; then on southward to the region of the Ten Towns, east and southeast of the Sea of Galilee. This wide detour brought him back to that lake without ever re-entering Galilee, the territory of Antipas. It cannot be doubted that Jesus made this wide circle because it was not yet safe for him to return. But a case of curing an unfortunate man there immediately made his presence known, in spite of his efforts to keep it secret; the more he forbade them, the more they spread the news far and wide.

CHAPTER XI

The Third Clash with the Pharisees

The boat had been brought across to him from his own side of the lake, and he took it, to a place called Dalmanutha, or as Matthew calls it Magadan—possibly Magdala, on the west shore of the lake. While neither of these places has been satisfactorily identified, the narrative seems to imply that he was once more in Galilee; the Pharisees immediately confronted him, demanding a sign to prove his right to teach such startling innovations as he had proposed in their last encounter.

By a sign they meant something as astonishing and convincing as the signs Moses was shown when he was called to become the deliverer and lawgiver of his people. They are related in Exodus, Chapter 4—his staff turning into a snake, and his hand turning leprous and then well again. Moses was told that, if these signs did not convince people of his divine mission, he could pour the water from the Nile on the ground, and it would turn into blood.

When Jesus swept aside the food regulations of Leviticus with a single sentence, he must, the Pharisees argued, work some such wonder as these to show his right to do it.

Jesus only sighed deeply, and refused.

"Why do men of this day ask for a sign?" he asked. "I tell you, no sign will be given them."

With these words he left them, and getting into the boat again he crossed to the other side of the lake, where he would be out of the dominion of Antipas.

As he and his disciples crossed the lake, to the vicinity of Bethsaida, he warned them against the leaven of the Pharisees, and of Herod. Matthew says that by this he meant their teaching, while Luke says it was their hypocrisy. They could not accept his acts of kindness and beneficence, his cures and exorcisms, as a sufficient sign; it must be some pointless, purposeless exhibition of power, like Moses' staff turning into a snake, or his hand turning leprous before their eyes. Besides, they believed their own rabbis could cast out demons and cure people, and the kind of sign they wanted must be more than that.

The disciples had forgotten to bring along any bread on this voyage, and fancied he was alluding to this omission on their part. But he speedily corrected that impression. Why should they worry about bread after what they had witnessed at the feeding of the five thousand?

At Bethsaida he cured a blind man, and sent him straight to his home, telling him not even to go into the neighboring village. He himself led his disciples north from Bethsaida to the neighborhood of Caesarea Philippi, where he had touched on his recent journey back from Tyre and Sidon. This is his third retreat before his Galilean foes, who he clearly saw were so offended at his saying that what a man ate did not affect his standing with

God that they were resolved with the aid of their agents in Antipas' circle to destroy him.

Jesus spent some days among the villages around Caesarea Philippi, for the most part in close conference with his disciples, the faithful twelve. He questioned them closely as to what the people among whom they had gone about so widely thought about him, and in particular who they thought he was. They gave him various answers. Some, they said, thought he was John the Baptist, restored to life; others that he was Elijah, brought back, as Malachi had foretold, as the messenger of God's covenant, the forerunner of the terrible day of the Lord's judgment and vindication. Still others, they said, thought he was some other one of the old prophets, or perhaps even a new prophet altogether, in line with the old promise of Moses, in Deuteronomy 18:15.

Then he put the question to them, personally. Who did they think he was? What did they consider his role in the great drama of Israel's religion to be?

"But who do you say that I am?"

What part did they think he was to play, what place was he to take in the progress of religion? It was no mere intelligence test; he was actually consulting them. He was weighing his own future course. The peaceful, tranquil evangelization of the masses was now belligerently blocked by the Pharisees, who with their connections at court had it in their power to put him out of the way, if he went on. They had now taken the offensive in Galilee, calling upon him for a sign from heaven, if he was to teach such subversive things. He must find a new avenue of approach to the people, or he would be snuffed out as John had been, obscurely, in a prison cell, with his work only begun.

It was Peter who made bold to answer.

"You are the Christ!"

Jesus' immediate response was to warn them all not to say this about him to anyone. But Matthew declares that he welcomed the designation, and commended Peter for his answer in the strongest terms. It was now, according to the Gospel of Matthew, that Jesus named Simon Cephas, the Aramaic word for rock, and so in Greek tradition Simon came to be known as Petros—in English, Peter. Of course the two statements are not at all inconsistent; Jesus may well have welcomed Peter's loyal recognition of his title to the great Messianic role, interpreted as he proposed to interpret it, and at the same time have charged them all to keep it absolutely to themselves for the present. Mark in 3:16 refers to Jesus' giving the name Peter to Simon but does not say when or why. But Matthew proceeds,

"On this rock," meaning no doubt the rock of his own Messiahship, "I will build my church," that is, form my new religious society, "and the powers of death shall not subdue it!"

The term *Christ*, or in Hebrew *Messiah*, means anointed, and primarily suggested someone of the princely line of David, rightful heir to his throne. It had also come to be applied to anyone with a supposedly divine commission, anointed with the spirit, as the prophets were, as in

Isaiah 61:1. Currently, it was sometimes appropriated by leaders of revolutionary movements, designed to cast off the Roman yoke and re-establish political independence. A term so flexible was fraught with great danger to anyone who assumed it, or even accepted it, for it sounded to Roman authority like a signal for rebellion. To proclaim himself as Messiah might win Jewish attention for Jesus and his message, but it would bring down swift Roman vengeance. Before he accepted the title and made it serve his work and purpose, Jesus was careful to reinterpret it for his closest disciples, so that there would be no uncertainty in their minds about it, as applied to him. That was to be the meaning of the Transfiguration, where they later came to see him with Moses and Elijah, the great molders of their religion. It was to that order that he belonged.

Jesus now began to tell his disciples that the Son of Man, as he called himself, must go through great suffering and be rejected by the leaders of the people, and killed, though he recalled Hosea's prediction of revival and resurrection, in two or three days. This was terrible news to the hitherto hopeful and enthusiastic band. Peter saw in it signs of weakening before the great Messianic role, and began to reprove him for it. But he answered with terrible sternness,

"Get out of my sight, you Satan! You do not side with God, but with men!"

The passion in these words reveal the emotional anguish that the prospect caused him. What he needed was strength to face the fearful ordeal before him, not encouragement to blind himself to it. As it was, it spurred him to his irrevocable decision. He called the people and his disciples to him and said to them,

"If anyone wants to go with me, he must disregard himself and take his cross and follow me!" This was a grim prospect for the little group of peaceable, earnest young Galileans, so eager to serve God and help their fellow-men. They knew only too well what taking up a cross meant; Varus only thirty years before had crucified two thousand Jews in one campaign. But Jesus went on,

"Whoever wants to preserve his own life will lose it, and whoever loses his life for me and for the good news, will preserve it." They were entering a stage in their work that would put them to a terrible test.

"If anyone is ashamed of me and my teaching in this unfaithful and sinful age, then the Son of Man will be ashamed of him when he comes back in his Father's glory, with the holy angels." For visions of eventual certain triumph rose before him. "I tell you some of you who stand here, will certainly live to see the reign of God come in its might!"

Jesus to some extent shared the current view of his times that God would eventually rebuke human wickedness and Satan's rule of the world, apocalyptically, that is, by an overwhelming exhibition of his power in the judgment and reformation of mankind. This is really no more than to say that men cannot go on forever disobeying God and doing wrong. God's kingdom is eventually going to prevail, he is really going to reign. But Jesus did not postpone the kingdom to that vague and distant "day of the Lord"; he proposed that men recognize God's reign here and now, and live as individuals under its sway. The kingdom of God, he said to them, is among you, or within you; in either case it is a present reality. Jesus was well aware that God's violent triumph through an apocalyptic judgment would not be the noblest triumph for God's cause; its noblest triumph would be won only through winning the hearts of men to the will of God. But of the success of that undertaking he was sure; the Son of Man would indeed come back, in his Father's glory, with the holy angels. It is his bold, imaginative way of asserting the certain triumph of the kingdom of God he was establishing among them.

As we have seen, *Son of Man* in the gospels sometimes means (as in Aramaic) simply man, as in Psalm 8:4; sometimes Jesus himself, as Ezekiel used it of himself so often—"mortal man"; and sometimes the Messianic agent of the establishment of the kingdom of God. But just when the second of these senses blends with the third it is sometimes difficult to decide.

The week that followed must have seen great searchings of heart on the part of the twelve, as they pondered on these solemn and portentous words. One afternoon Jesus took Peter, who had ventured to question the program, with James and John, who formed with him an inner confidential circle within the group, on a long walk, and led them up on a mountain to pray. There they had an extraordinary experience. As he prayed, Jesus seemed to become a supernatural being, his clothes dazzling white, and Elijah and Moses stood beside him, and talked with him.

Peter was the one who had needed convincing, and he is the ancient authority for the experience, and the one most clearly convinced by it. For he broke in upon the scene to say, in his confusion,

"Master, how good it is that we are here! Let us put up three booths, one for you and one for Moses and one for Elijah!"

A cloud, bright like the emblem of the divine presence, overshadowed them, and Peter seemed to hear a heavenly voice say,

"This is my Son, my Beloved! Listen to him!"

Then suddenly, as he looked around, he found no one with them but Jesus. But the experience had taught Peter a great lesson, for he had seen Jesus not with the old kings of Israel, or with its captains, but with the great framers of its religion, Moses the lawgiver, and Elijah the re-founder of the prophetic order. Jesus cautioned them to tell nobody about it, until the Son of Man should be risen from the dead.

Whatever we may think of the transfiguration experience, and however we may understand it, it certainly gave the inner circle of apostles, or at least Peter, a new conception of the mission and stature of Jesus, and of his Messianic role. He was now seen to be not a political or military but a great religious Messiah, whose work was not with Israel's politics but with its religion. His predecessors were not kings and warriors, like David or Judas Maccabeus, but prophets and lawgivers. Most interestingly Jesus instructs them to say nothing of this to the other nine or anyone else, until, as Mark puts it, the Son of Man should rise from the dead. Jesus does not wish his Messiahship discussed until he has had his own opportunity at Jerusalem to show its character.

As they went down the mountain, they asked him why the scribes said Elijah had to come before the Messiah made his appearance.

"Elijah does come first," he answered, "and reforms everything, and does not the scripture say of the Son of Man that he will suffer much and be refused? Why, I tell you, not only has Elijah come, but people have treated him just as they pleased, as the scripture says about him!"

This was clearly an identification of John the Baptist with the returned Elijah. And clearly enough, Jesus' own conception of the Messiah—his "Son of Man"—here is the Suffering Servant of the Book of Isaiah, a conception that had already colored his use of Isaiah, Chapter 61, in the synagogue at Nazareth. It must be remembered, too, that Jewish Messianic thought had never taken these great chapters to refer to the Messiah. As Dr. Fosdick puts it, "The identification of Christ in the New Testament with Isaiah's Suffering Servant was a startling innovation" (*The Man from Nazareth*, p. 122).

This significant episode, with its attendant conversations, probably took place on some spur of the Hermon range, above Caesarea Philippi, where Jesus had taken temporary refuge, outside of Galilee, from the machina-

tions of the Pharisees and their Herodian sympathizers.
There he faced the question of his next step in his work.
To return to Galilee was to court speedy destruction, with
his mission to the unchurched masses of Galilee only
begun. Ever since the Pharisees of Galilee had first threatened him, he had been taking measures to perpetuate his
work through his disciples, in case of his death, as Isaiah
had done. But he had no mind to die obscurely in some
corner of Galilee, to no purpose. A bolder plan was now
taking shape in his mind. He would present himself in
Jerusalem, the stronghold of the priesthood and the
Sadducees, and at the temple itself, before the people
gathered at their great festival, the Passover, publicly offer
them their Messianic destiny, and take the consequences.
And he would do this in ways that would make his death
something that would never be forgotten, but would carry
on his message to the end of time. Yet how could this be
done?

We cannot indeed look into his mind in these fateful
days in the villages around Caesarea Philippi, but his
actions from this point onward show us his great purpose.
And to the last night of his life he did not wholly give up
the hope of succeeding at Jerusalem, and really winning
the victory with his people.

His overwhelming inner urge to relieve the miseries of
those about him finds expression again as they rejoin the
disciples. To the agonized father of the epileptic boy,
Jesus says,

"Everything is possible for one who has faith!"

With unspeakable pathos, the man cries out,
"I have faith! Help my want of faith!"

The story is told with the convincing detail of an eye-witness. I have seen just such a wretched child writhing on the ground in a village street in Palestine.

Jesus' plans are now, we must believe, formed. But he first leads the twelve back to Capernaum, and as they go through northern Galilee he again warns the disciples of what lies before him. He is to be handed over to men who will kill him, but after three days he will rise again. This hope recalls Hosea's words, 6:1, 2:

> "He smote, but he will bind us up;
> He will revive us in two or three days;
> He will raise us up that we may live before him."

So at last they reached home in Capernaum again. There he asked them what they had been discussing on their long walk. They would not tell, because they had been discussing which of them was the greatest. He sat down to teach, and called them before him.

"If anyone wishes to be first," he said, "he must be the last of all and the servant of all."

We do not always realize how fully Jesus himself exemplified his ideal of humility; President Ernest C. Colwell, in his *Approach to the Teaching of Jesus*, finds that "the supreme tribute to Jesus' own humility is that no one can answer the question, 'What did Jesus think of himself?'"

Almost as though anxious to change the subject, John

said to him, "Master, we saw a man driving out demons with your name, and we told him not to do so, for he was not one of our followers."

But Jesus said,

"Do not tell him not to do so. A man who is not against us is for us. For whoever gives you a cup of water to drink on the ground that you belong to Christ, I tell you, will certainly not fail to be repaid. Whoever causes one of these humble believers to fall might better have a great millstone hung around his neck and be thrown into the sea!"

It was probably from such rigorous acts as John admitted that Jesus nicknamed him and his brother "Sons of Thunder."

"Beware," Jesus went on, "of feeling scornful of one single little child, for I tell you that in heaven their angels have continual access to my Father in heaven!"

They must not cherish misunderstandings with one another, but be quick to seek reconciliation. Peter inquired, perhaps a little ironically,

"Master, how many times am I to forgive my brother when he wrongs me? Seven times over?"

Jesus would not permit the duty of forgiveness to be reduced to a calculated rule. He answered,

"Not seven times over, I tell you, but seventy-seven times over."

Jesus took unforgiving old Lamech's ratio of revenge, Genesis 4:24—any wrong done him he would avenge seventy-seven fold—and made it the ratio of forgiveness!

He went on to tell them the searching story of the Unforgiving Debtor.

Anything now in their lives that would impair their religious development must be ruthlessly pruned away; hand, foot, eye—none of these things, however precious, must be retained if it menaced their entry into life. The reference to Gehenna—the Valley of Hinnom where the refuse of Jerusalem was thrown—reflects Jeremiah's use of the phrase, and shows again how full Jesus' mind was of the great prophets. The sinister allusions to salt and fire as purifying elements show that Jesus was preparing his disciples for his next step, which might prove such a fearful test of their devotion.

CHAPTER XII

The Great Offensive:
Jesus Moves on Jerusalem

Thus far Jesus had worked only in Galilee, that stirring, populous, busy district, trying to reach the religiously neglected masses, the people of the land, of whom Pharisaism frankly despaired. But three times in a few months he had been threatened by the Pharisees and temporarily halted in this work. How real his peril was, the recent fate of John the Baptist only too clearly showed. The Pharisees could easily bring about his own death through their alliance with Herod's partisans. But to die obscurely in some corner of Galilee would accomplish nothing. Jesus had now highly resolved that if he must indeed give his life for his cause he would do it in a way that would not terminate his work but perpetuate it. And yet he was not without hope of winning the Jewish people to his side. At their great annual feast he would present himself to them, wipe out the wrongs that oppressed them, and offer them their great Messianic destiny, the moral and religious leadership of mankind. They might accept it and indeed set up the kingdom of God on earth. It was his deepest hope that they would do so. But if they did not, and he must pay for his effort with his life, he would do so in a manner which should forever commemorate his great undertaking, and make his message remembered long after he was gone. He would create a memory that should be eternal. The proof of this is the historical fact that he did so! This was surely no accident.

Mark reports, and we remember that he is speaking for Peter, that Jesus left Capernaum and went into the district of Judea, and crossed the Jordan. Between Galilee and Judea lay Samaria, which Jews generally avoided, preferring to make the journey from Galilee to Jerusalem by crossing into Perea, on the east bank of the river, a part of the modern Trans-Jordan. Jesus was evidently following that route to the capital; it was the natural course for him and his disciples to take, and besides it would take them to Jerusalem along with the hordes of people on their way to the festival of the Passover. As he went, crowds of people again gathered about him, and again he taught them as he was accustomed to do.

But Trans-Jordan, like Galilee, was governed by Herod Antipas, and the Pharisees were immediately at Jesus' heels again. They had their grapevine, their channels of intercommunication, and they were ready for him. They came to him ostensibly to learn; at least to get his opinion on a divisive, much debated question: Could a man divorce his wife? Of course, the Jewish Law of Deuteronomy said plainly that he could; if she did not please him, because he had found some indecency in her, he could divorce her simply by drawing up a notice of divorce and giving it to her. Even this had been an advance upon the cruel and barbarous state of things before Deuteronomy was discovered and became the law, in 621 B.C. Thereafter the poor woman had a document vouching for her respectability, at least, and was free to marry again. And of course, as Deuteronomy was popularly ascribed to Moses, its ostensible author, it was commonly spoken of as his legislation. The question arose, however: What was meant by an indecency? Shammai, in the days of King Herod, said it meant unchastity, unfaithfulness to her husband, but Hillel, the leading authority in Jesus' boyhood (30 B.C.-A.D. 10), who summed up the Law in the negative Golden Rule, "What is hateful to thee, do not unto thy fellow-man," said it meant anything about her that displeased her husband, even putting too much salt in his soup, and Akiba (A.D. 50-135), the "father of Rabbinism," said if her husband found someone more attractive, he could divorce her. Indeed, by the end of the first century it was agreed that where Hillel and Shammai disagreed, Hillel was the authority to follow, and it is easy to see where this left Jewish womanhood. When the Pharisees asked Jesus their question, the position of woman in Judaism was on the way down, and going perilously lower. The Mishnah recognizes a man's right to have four or five wives, as Justin Martyr also states, in his *Dialogue with Trypho,* 134:1 (A.D. 155-60).

Jesus met the Pharisees' question by asking what Moses

commanded on the subject. They replied with the written divorce-notice provision. A man had only to draw one up, and he could divorce his wife forthwith.

Jesus handled the matter boldly. He quoted the creation story.

"It was on account of your perversity that he laid down that law for you. From the beginning of the creation, 'God made them male and female. Therefore a man must leave his father and mother and he and his wife must become one.'" And Jesus added, "And so they are no longer two, but one. Therefore what God has joined together man must not try to separate."

There is tremendous insight here into the union of husband and wife in the felicity of a true and lasting marriage. The Pharisees evidently had no more to say on the subject. But the disciples themselves were a good deal staggered by his decision, and when they reached the house where they were staying, and were by themselves, they asked him to explain.

"Anyone," he said, "who divorces his wife and marries another woman commits adultery against his former wife, and if a woman divorces her husband and marries another man, she is an adulteress!"

This was strong doctrine. It went beyond Shammai; beyond even Deuteronomy. Against them both Jesus appealed to the fundamental constitution of the marriage relation, as so nobly expressed in the creation story. He had an amazing understanding of the deep bond that unites husband and wife in a true marriage, and appealed to that, as it appeared in the creation narrative. It was indeed a sublime expression of the basic contract in human relations; there is nothing more fundamental in society. Yet how slowly has civilization since advanced toward this ideal. Certainly he left contemporary Judaism far behind when he said this. Yet Jesus was no mere petty legislator; he was laying down the great ideals of life, the vision of all that it might be and ought to be. As he said once to a man who questioned him about his personal rights, "Who made me a judge or arbitrator of your affairs?"

As they continued on their way through Trans-Jordan, people brought their children to him, to have him touch them. The disciples, accustomed to regard children as insignificant, reproved them for doing so. But when Jesus observed this, he was indignant, and said to them,

"Let the children come to me; do not try to stop them, for the kingdom of God belongs to such as they. I tell you, whoever does not accept the kingdom of God like a child, shall not enter it at all!"

Then he took the children in his arms, and laid his hands on them and blessed them. This respect and concern for childhood was as amazing in his day as his concern for womanhood. In the Roman world, unwanted babies, especially if they were girls, were thrown out to die; a Greek papyrus of the year 1 B.C. from an absent husband to his wife in Oxyrhynchus gives her specific instructions to this effect. Such abandoned babies were often picked up by slave dealers and brought up for the slave market; Hermas, the Christian prophet of Rome, about A.D. 100, had gone through that experience.

Jesus was advancing new views of human personality, with tremendous social implications. He had said once, probably while still in Galilee,

"Beware of feeling scornful of one single little child, for I tell you that in heaven their angels have continual access to my Father in heaven!" He went on to tell them a story of a shepherd with a hundred sheep, who lost one of them, and left the ninety-nine on the hills while he went in search of it. When he found it, he was happier about it than he was about the other ninety-nine, who were safe where he had left them. So much, Jesus thought, the individual mattered. So for the wife, the child, the individual, Jesus was greatly concerned. He saw their need and their importance, and stood up for them, in a most neglectful age, and a most neglectful world, too, for it still has much to learn from him of its responsibility for all three.

It was all just a part of Jesus' great concern for human misery, not only the sick, the crippled or the mad, but the neglected, the lonely, the misunderstood. Human suffering, physical, mental, emotional, commanded his concern and help.

One of those attracted by him on his way was a rich young man, who was interested in his preaching of the kingdom of God, and came up and knelt at his feet to ask him how he could make sure of eternal life. When he assured Jesus of his lifelong obedience to the Ten Commandments, Jesus loved him, and said to him,

"There is one thing that you lack; go and sell all you have, and give the money to the poor, and then you will have riches in heaven; and come back and be a follower of mine."

This was too much for the young man, for he was rich, and very much attached to his property, and he went away in great dejection. Jesus remarked how hard it was for rich men to get into the kingdom of God. This seemed strange to the disciples; they had supposed the rich were the very ones who would find it easiest to get into it. They had money to give away, and did not have to do all the defiling things that poor men could not escape. But he repeated his remark, and added, in his inimitable rhetoric,

"It is easier for a camel to get through the eye of a needle than for a rich man to get into the kingdom of God!"

The disciples were astounded, and said to him,

"Then who can be saved?" To the Pharisaic mind, the religious mind of the time, this was one of the advantages of wealth; it enabled one to observe the Law.

He answered,

"For men it is impossible, but not for God, for anything is possible for God."

Peter started to tell him how they had left all they had to follow him, and he answered,

"I tell you, there is no one who has given up home or

brothers or sisters or mother or father or children or land for me and the good news but will receive now in this life a hundred times as much in homes, brothers, sisters, mothers, children, and lands—though not without persecution—and in the coming age eternal life. But many who are first now will be last then, and the last will be first."

CHAPTER XIII

The Advance Through Trans-Jordan

Jesus must have made no haste in his journey through Trans-Jordan to Jerusalem, for Luke records a whole series of incidents and teachings connected with this journey; they constitute the largest part of the Gospel of Luke that seems to owe nothing to the Gospel of Mark, but to be drawn from another record. It forms Luke 9:51 to 18:14 and 19:1-28, or almost one-third of Luke's gospel, and while its narratives probably do not form a continuous record, they preserve much that is undoubtedly historical, even though we may not be able to fix their place definitely in the action of Jesus' ministry. Indeed, not a few of them may have taken place in Galilee.

That he should have touched Samaritan soil in passing from Galilee into Perea is likely enough, though this is probably not the meaning of Luke, who more than once speaks of him as journeying through Samaria, on his final journey to Jerusalem (9:52; 17:11). The messengers he sent ahead to one village where he planned to spend the night were refused accommodation by the villagers, because Jesus and his party were bound for Jerusalem, and the feeling between Jews and Samaritans was very strongly hostile. Those sons of thunder James and John thought the villagers should be made an example of, by being consumed with fire from heaven, as Elijah consumed the soldiers sent to arrest him—II Kings 1:10, 12. Jesus merely reproved them for their fierce demand, and they went on to another village.

One day, as they were on their way, a man said to Jesus,

"I will follow you wherever you go!"

Jesus answered,

"Foxes have holes, and wild birds have nests, but the Son of Man has nowhere to lay his head!" He has no home; the man must understand that. He would seem to have embarked upon the decisive stage of his enterprise, just as Luke places it; he has set his face toward Jerusalem.

To another he said,

"Follow me!"

But the man had an excuse for procrastination:

"Let me first go and bury my father"—that is, see him through his old age to the end of his days.

Jesus said to him,

"Leave the dead to bury their own dead! You must go and spread the news of the kingdom of God!" He was offering the man a higher duty even than that to his parents.

Another man said to him,

"Master, I am going to follow you, but let me first say goodbye to my people at home."

Jesus said to him,

"No one who puts his hand to the plough, and then looks back, is fitted for the kingdom of God."

Jesus shows a great sense of urgency in these responses, as well he might, if, as Luke puts it, he had set his face toward Jerusalem. Now was when the kingdom needed to muster all its strength, if it was to succeed at Jerusalem.

The sending of messengers ahead to arrange entertainment for his party must be the explanation of Luke's account of the seventy-two whom he now sent before him; it is clear that he had a number of people with him besides the twelve; the later narrative speaks of the women who followed him from Galilee, and as the head of this delegation on its way to the Passover he would naturally want to insure accommodations ahead. Of course these messengers would have to give some explanation of who it was who was approaching with such a following. And Jesus may well have wished to approach Jerusalem at the head of a peaceful body of followers that had grown on its way through Trans-Jordan to great proportions. We may well suppose that the arrangements so carefully made for the colt on which Jesus was to ride into Jerusalem, and the upstairs room in Jerusalem where he could eat the Passover with his disciples, were made through some of these emissaries (Mark 11:2, 3; 14:12-16).

As the choosing of the twelve has a parallel in Isaiah's circle of disciples, the sending out of the seventy-two recalls Moses' appointment of seventy, or with Eldad and Medad seventy-two, elders (Numbers 11:16-25), though of course their function was quite different.

The seventy-two messengers were sent out in pairs, so

that if each pair went to a different place, Jesus must have mapped out a series of thirty-six towns and villages through which he planned to pass on his journey southward. If he proposed to spend a night in each, this would involve a journey of six weeks, for his party would hardly travel on the Sabbath. That he contemplated any such prolonged tour through Samaria is improbable; he had told the twelve when he had sent them out not to visit Samaritan towns. Pursuing his own idea of working among his own people, so emphasized in Matthew, he would find them in what the gospels speak of as "Across Jordan," exactly as we now call the same region (though much enlarged) "Trans-Jordan," from the Latin Vulgate "Trans Jordanem," rather than in Samaria. Any Jews from Galilee going to the festival in his train would certainly prefer not to go through Samaria, if they did not positively refuse to do so. So his route must have been through Trans-Jordan.

The seventy-two returned to him delighted with their reception and their success. He shared their enthusiasm. "I saw Satan fall from heaven like a flash of lightning!" he cried. He had found the key, the weapon for evil's overthrow. Joy and gratitude filled his heart and he uttered an impassioned thanksgiving:

"I thank you, Father, Lord of heaven and earth, for hiding all this from the learned and intelligent, and revealing it to children! Yes, I thank you, Father, for choosing to have it so!

"Everything has been handed over to me by my Father,

and no one knows who the Son is but the Father, nor who the Father is but the Son and anyone to whom the Son chooses to reveal him!"

When they were alone, he said to his disciples,

"Blessed are the eyes that see what you see! For I tell you, many prophets and kings have wished to see what you see, and could not see it, and to hear what you hear, and could not hear it!"

All this sounds very much as though it was uttered just as Luke says it was, on the way up to Jerusalem, where he proposed to put his campaign to the final test, before the Jewish people, gathered in their historic capital for their great annual festival.

At one of their stopping places, an expert in the Law, doubtless a Pharisee, tried to involve him in debate.

"Master," said he, "what must I do to make sure of eternal life?"

Jesus asked him what the Law said about it. He replied,

" 'You must love the Lord your God with your whole heart, your whole soul, your whole strength and your whole mind,' and 'your neighbor as you do yourself.' "

This was that fourfold love, including one's whole mind, which Jesus himself so emphasized, though the great Jewish Shema ("Listen"), in Deuteronomy 6:5, is usually understood to mean, "all your heart, soul and strength." Jesus assured him he was right; if he did that he would live. Still anxious to find a point of difference with Jesus, the questioner went on,

"And who is my neighbor?"

Jesus answered him with the parable of the Good Samaritan, which a modern philanthropist has declared to be the noblest and most characteristic expression of the Christian religion. The Jericho road, which lay ahead of them on their way to Jerusalem, was notorious for the robbers who infested it. A man on his way from Jerusalem to Jericho had been robbed and beaten by some of these miscreants and left half-dead on the roadside. Passers-by paid no attention to the poor man's plight, but hurried on about their business. A priest, trudging along, took the other side of the road. So did a traveling Levite. Perhaps they wanted to escape the risk of defilement in touching a possibly dead body, which would by the law of Numbers 19:11 have made them unclean, and so incapable of performing their official duties about the temple for at least a week. They were religious professionals. It was a traveling Samaritan, a member of a detested sect, that really pitied the man and looked after him, binding up his wounds and taking him to an inn where he could be nursed back to health—even providing for his subsequent care. So it was the Samaritan who showed himself the real neighbor of the wounded Jew; he knew that true humanity knows no barriers of race or creed, when one's fellow-creatures are in distress.

In a village which may have been Bethany, though that is far from likely, Jesus was entertained by a woman named Martha, who thought her sister Mary was much more interested in listening to his teaching than in helping her with the housework. But Jesus thought women were worth talking to about religion, and said his teaching was really the most important thing of all, and Mary was not wrong in listening to it. It was a time, he felt, for great decisions.

It was on this anxious yet hopeful journey to Jerusalem that Luke places the origin of the Lord's Prayer, which Matthew incorporates into the Sermon on the Mount. We have spoken of it in connection with John the Baptist, for Luke states that once when Jesus had been praying, his disciples said to him,

"Master, teach us to pray, as John taught his disciples."

He responded at once with the prayer we know so well, but in a shorter form than Matthew's; he said to them,

"When you pray, say, 'Father, your name be revered! Your kingdom come! Give us each day our bread for the day, and forgive us our sins, for we ourselves forgive anyone who wrongs us; and do not subject us to temptation.' "

He went on to tell them the inimitable story of the neighbor coming in the middle of the night to borrow three loaves of bread, because a friend has just come to his house after a journey, and he has nothing for him to eat. The man thus rudely broken of his rest replies not unnaturally,

"Do not bother me; the door is now fastened, and my children and I have gone to bed. I cannot get up and give you any."

Nevertheless, when the neighbor persists in his entreaties and will not go away, the man will at last get up and give him all he needs. The lesson of this quaint and even humorous story is, they must be persistent and determined in their prayers:

"Ask, and what you ask will be given you. Search, and you will find what you search for. Knock, and the door will open to you."

The old charge that he drives out the demons by the aid of Beelzebub the prince of the demons, calls forth a stern rebuke. If Beelzebub is helping to cast out demons, his kingdom is collapsing beneath him. But if it is with God's help that Jesus is casting them out, then the kingdom of God has overtaken them! It has caught up with them, it has arrived.

A woman in the crowd calls down God's blessing upon his mother, but he corrects her; his mother had not encouraged him in his task.

"You might better say, 'Blessed are those who hear God's message and observe it.'"

Even in Trans-Jordan crowds gathered to hear him speak, and he warned them against demanding a sign from him. Jonah's preaching was the only sign the men of Nineveh needed to make them repent, in the Jonah story, and they will rise up in the judgment with the men of this generation and condemn them, for they repented at Jonah's preaching, but there is something greater than Jonah here. The Greek does not mean "someone greater," it is neuter, "something greater," meaning the kingdom of God.

A great deal of Jesus' teaching in Luke's Trans-Jordan section, 9:51-18:14, and 19:1-28, reminds the reader of the more familiar Sermon on the Mount, suggesting that both Matthew and Luke have had, in addition to Mark, the use of the same document as a source, which Luke seems to have presented more as he found it than Matthew did. This is very probable, for Matthew used Mark more freely than Luke did.

The seventy-two heralds of his coming had evidently made contacts with some leading Pharisees along the way through Trans-Jordan, for he was occasionally hospitably entertained by Pharisees on this journey—11:37; 14:1. It was one of these hospitable men who was so surprised that Jesus did not wash before eating with him. Jesus pointed out to him that externality was the Pharisees' characteristic mistake, but it was the inner life that mattered, in the sight of God. The incident strikingly confirms Mark's picture of Jewish usage, in Mark 7:2, 3.

An expert in the Law spoke up in defense of the Pharisee.

"Master, when you say that, you affront us too."

Jesus accepted the man's challenge.

"Yes, alas for you experts in the Law, too! For you load men with burdens they can hardly carry, and you will not touch them yourselves with a single finger." Jesus points to their attitude toward the prophets; the only prophets they recognize are the dead prophets; they are willing to build tombs for dead prophets, but not to listen to living ones. As a matter of fact, their position was that the voice of prophecy had ceased in the time of Ezra, about 400 B.C. They had taken the key to the door of knowledge; they would not enter it themselves, and they kept out those who tried to enter—that is, they had smothered the great principles of prophetic religion under a mass of trivial technicalities.

This outspoken rebuke of both Pharisees and experts in the Law led the scribes and Pharisees to watch Jesus more closely and to try to entrap him into some even more unguarded and outspoken criticism of their views. His reference to the murder of Zechariah right in the temple itself, as given in Luke 11:51, is evidently to the incident of the stoning of Zechariah the son of Jehoiada the priest, in the court of the house of the Lord, related in II Chronicles 24:20, 21. It was the last murder recorded in their great series of historical books, from Genesis to Chronicles, as that of Abel in Genesis 4:8 was the first. Their present generation, Jesus said, would be charged with all the murders in their history, because it refused to repent and reform.

This clash with the scribes and Pharisees was quickly noised abroad and a great crowd gathered, some taking the side of the Pharisee, and some that of Jesus. Jesus pursued the subject with his disciples, assuring them that hypocrisy was futile, as the truth was inevitably destined to come out, and urging them to courageous sincerity, in whatever circumstances. Persecution might tempt them to hypocrisy, but they had better fear God rather than men. His care would not fail them; it included even the tiniest birds. They must not fear or fail to acknowledge him before men, even if brought before synagogues or magistrates to account for their views.

This serious admonition was interrupted by a voice from

the crowd. A man spoke up begging him to tell his brother to give him his rightful share of their inheritance. But Jesus refused to be drawn into a mere quarrel between two greedy men.

"Who made me a judge or arbitrator of your affairs?" he asked, and turning to the crowd, he went on,

"Take care! You must be on your guard against any form of greed, for a man's life does not belong to him, no matter how rich he is!"

Then he told them this story:

"A certain rich man's lands yielded heavily. And he said to himself, 'What am I going to do, for I have nowhere to store my crops? This is what I will do; I will tear down my barns and build larger ones, and in them I will store all my grain and my goods. And I will say to my soul, Soul, you have great wealth stored up for years to come. Now take your ease; eat, drink, and enjoy yourself!' But God said to him, 'You fool! This very night your soul will be demanded of you. Then who will have all you have prepared?' That is the way with the man who lays up money for himself, and is not rich with God."

He told his disciples not to worry about the necessaries of life; God fed even the crows! How much more they were worth than the birds! Their first endeavor must be to find his kingdom. He knows full well how divisive his work may prove; it will set father against son, and son against father—a reminiscence of his own home experience.

In Trans-Jordan a story was brought to Jesus of Pilate's bloody violence to some pilgrims from Galilee (resembling what Josephus relates in *Antiquities* xviii.3. 2), perhaps in the hope that it would rouse him to indignant revolt, but he finds in it, and a similar disaster at Siloam, only a fresh call for repentance. He goes on his way curing the sick and uttering new parables—the Unfruitful Fig Tree, the Tiny Mustard Seed, the Yeast That Raised the Dough.

Not all the Pharisees, at least in Trans-Jordan, were hostile to Jesus; some of them even warned him of his peril. Someone had asked him whether only a few would be saved, a question much discussed among the Jews, as in II Esdras 8:1-3, and he replied with the parable of the late-comers reaching their host's house too late to be admitted. The door is narrow, and men cannot take their own time about entering it. The Jews who thought themselves sure of admittance would see people from the east and west and north and south taking their places side by side with Abraham, Isaac and Jacob and all the prophets, in the kingdom of God, while they were put outside.

"There are those now last," he concluded, "who will then be first, and there are those now first who will be last!"

Just then, Luke goes on, some Pharisees came up, and said to him,

"Go! Get away from here, for Herod wants to kill you!"

Mark has shown that the Pharisees were in touch with Herod's agents up in Galilee, and now in Trans-Jordan Jesus was still in the territory of Herod Antipas.

It was probably from their Pharisaic connections that these men knew what they did of Jesus' danger, but they understood Jesus better, and were conscious of a basic agreement with him. It is a curious confirmation, from quite another source, of the dangers Mark repeatedly mentions as threatening him in Galilee from the Pharisees and the minions of Antipas.

Jesus replied with vigor.

"Go and say to that fox, 'Here I am, driving out demons, and performing cures, today and tomorrow, and on the third day I will be through. But I must go on today and tomorrow and the next day, for it is not right for a prophet to die outside Jerusalem.' " And it was now, Luke declares, that he uttered his touching lament over Jerusalem, which Matthew postpones to the very end:

"O Jerusalem! Jerusalem! murdering the prophets, and stoning those who are sent to her, how often I have longed to gather your children around me, as a hen gathers her brood under her wings, but you refused!"

At a Pharisee's table, where he was entertained, he saw the eagerness of some of the guests to get the best places at table, and frankly warned them against such conduct:

"Everyone who exalts himself will be humbled, but the man who humbles himself will be exalted." How true it was to prove in his own case, and in the cases of countless followers of his, from Paul on.

He told them when they gave a dinner not to ask their relatives and their rich neighbors, but the poor, the maimed, the lame and the blind, who could never repay them with return invitations. One is reminded of Ecclesiasticus, and Ben Sirach's advice about conduct at dinners, so much more worldly-wise.

The difficulty of many of the sayings given in this section of Luke as uttered on the way through Trans-Jordan to Jerusalem is strong evidence of their genuineness, as preserving the words of Jesus. His great concern for the individual comes out strikingly in the parables of the Lost Sheep (the Ninety and Nine), and the Lost Coin. But even these fall into the background before the great story of the Prodigal Son, which is preserved only in Luke, and in this narrative of the journey through Trans-Jordan. It is followed by the startling story of the Dishonest Manager, who was threatened with discharge and took the opportunity to settle with his master's debtors on terms very favorable to them, in the hope of getting business opportunities from them after his approaching discharge. So they were to use their ill-gotten wealth to make friends for themselves in another world.

The story of the Rich Man and Lazarus follows, and then the short, moving one of the Pharisee and the Tax Collector. The Pharisee's prayer was full of complacency; he was glad of his superiority, and his virtue. But the tax collector stood at a distance, and would not even raise his eyes to heaven, but struck his breast and said,

"O God, have mercy on a sinner like me!"

Jesus said it was he that went back to his house with God's approval, and not the other, because everyone who exalted himself would be humbled, but the man who humbled himself would be exalted.

These three short stories, the Good Samaritan, the Prodigal Son and the Pharisee and the Tax Collector, are among the very greatest in the long list of Jesus' parables, and have found their places among the highest expressions of the Christian faith. They illustrate the amazing wealth and variety, and the unfailing vigor, of his teaching. The number of his parables that are preserved in the gospels has been variously estimated at from twenty-seven to fifty-nine! Most of us would reckon them at about forty. It is interesting to see how many of them one can remember, at least by name. Some are as short as a single verse; some occupy a whole page in a modern translation. Certainly they possessed and still possess a vividness and appeal that more didactic forms of teaching could not equal. And no other form of teaching was so characteristic of Jesus. No doubt he uttered scores of others which have been lost.

As we reflect upon this march through Trans-Jordan, and the step Jesus had taken to interest the townspeople along the way in his message, we cannot avoid the conclusion that he hoped great things from this mission on which he had sent the seventy-two, and on which he followed them. It seems as though he hoped that he and his messengers would be able to arouse sufficient popular support for his cause to make a peaceful invasion of Jerusalem by enough of his supporters to carry the day at the temple and really set up the kingdom of heaven on earth, not politically, but practically, in the hearts and lives of Judaism. The reports of his messengers gave him great encouragement; he began to feel that success was in sight, and so expressed himself in the cry of gratitude to God, in

Luke 10:21, 22, when he turned to his disciples and said,
"Blessed are the eyes that see what you see! For I tell
you, many prophets and kings have wished to see what you
see, and could not see it, and to hear what you hear, and
could not hear it!"

CHAPTER XIV

Jesus Reaches Jerusalem

As their journey through Trans-Jordan continued, a change came over Jesus. His old companionable manner gave way to one of abstraction and absorption. He strode on ahead of them alone, wrapped in his own thoughts. They were dismayed by this change, so unlike his old approachability, and such as still followed their group were positively afraid. At length he took the twelve apostles aside and again began to tell them what they might expect in Jerusalem, and what he had reason to suppose would happen to him there.

"See!" he said, "we are going up to Jerusalem, and the Son of Man will be handed over to the high priests and scribes, and they will condemn him to death, and hand him over to the heathen, and they will ridicule him and spit on him and flog him and kill him; and three days after he will rise again."

But this repetition of his former presentiment had little effect upon their hopefulness. How little was soon shown when James and John, jealous of Peter's manifest ascendancy, came to him with a bold, even a staggering request, which shows how confident they were of his success at Jerusalem.

"Master," they said, "we want you to do for us whatever we ask."

"What do you want me to do for you?" he asked.

They said to him,

"Let us sit one at your right hand and one at your left, in your triumph."

This was a startling demand, and its effect upon the other apostles may be imagined. And especially, where did it leave Peter, their leading spirit? The sons of Zebedee certainly thought well of themselves, and proposed to make the most of the great movement in which they felt themselves caught up. They had been almost the first disciples Jesus had called. And if they demanded much of the new movement, they were prepared to give all they had to give to it. But as yet they were looking upon it as preferment and fortune.

Jesus, on the other hand, was facing a dark and perilous prospect. He said to them,

"You do not know what you are asking for! Can you drink what I am drinking, or undergo the baptism I am undergoing?"

He was going through an agonizing experience, as he had tried to make them all see, and facing he knew not what consequences, and his answer must have sobered them, but they did not hesitate.

"Yes, we can," they answered.

He must have looked at them with compassion, for he said,

"Then you shall drink what I am drinking, and undergo the baptism that I am undergoing; but as for sitting at my right or at my left, that is not mine to give, but belongs to those for whom it is destined!"

Word of this extraordinary interview was not slow in reaching the rest of the twelve, and their first natural reaction was one of great indignation that the two brothers should have sought to steal a march upon them and get for themselves the chief places in the coming kingdom, to which they all evidently looked forward. They must have felt that Jesus could not fail in Jerusalem, but would unquestionably triumph, and place himself at the head of the Jewish people, if not politically at least religiously. The positions of his chief assistants or colleagues which James and John had asked for looked to them like places of great honor and authority in a brave new world.

Jesus called them all to him, and sought to set them right.

"You know," said he, "that those who are supposed to rule the heathen lord it over them, and their great men tyrannize over them, but it is not to be so among you. Whoever wants to be great among you must be your servant, and whoever wants to hold the first place among you must be everybody's slave. For the Son of Man himself has not come to be waited on, but to wait on other people, and to give his life to free many others."

This action of James and John reveals the optimism of the twelve as they made their way southward. But Jesus' mind was full of other and graver matters, as he planned his course in what he knew must be the momentous days at Jerusalem. They traveled probably not by the more di-

rect road that paralleled the river but by the higher one
that ran by way of Gilead through more settled country.
Jesus kept his own counsel, but it must have been now
that he was making the private arrangements that were
afterward to bear fruit when he reached Jerusalem, and
still later when he needed a room, in accordance with the
Law, within the city in which to eat the Passover. It is
significant that he felt these arrangements must be secretly
made, such was his sense of the peril that would hang over
him at the capital. This might have been arranged after he
was settled in the village of Bethany, half an hour out of
Jerusalem, though that too must have been arranged for
during this journey, for all the accommodations about the
city would be taken by the time his party arrived there.
But certainly the provision for an ass's colt, exactly such as
Zechariah had predicted the Messiah would some day
enter the city on, to be ready at the moment Jesus planned
to reach Jerusalem, surrounded by throngs of pilgrims to
the Passover, must have been made during this journey
through Trans-Jordan; that could not wait until his arrival. But Jesus clearly attached much importance to its
readiness. He is not going up to Jerusalem like a lamb to
the slaughter. He is making every effort beforehand to
dramatize his entry into the city and make it the keynote
of his great campaign there. The fact that he was coming
with only a few dozen disciples at his back, together with a
few women, only heightens the drama. Not only is he
hoping and striving to succeed; he has a course of action
in view to be followed in case of failure, that will he hopes

turn defeat into victory. All these considerations unite to make Jesus' visit to Jerusalem one of the most striking and significant narratives in history. It was at the very least the greatest week in the life of that city.

The journey through Trans-Jordan took perhaps six weeks, and on arriving opposite Judea Jesus' party doubtless recrossed the Jordan by the Roman bridge near Jericho and lodged there. As pilgrims to the festival they would be welcomed and provided for, even if Jesus' fame had not reached so far. But that it had done so is evident from the story of the curing of a blind beggar who sat by the roadside, as Jesus left the city for the last stage of his journey. Fifty years ago, we drove from Jerusalem to Jericho, by carriage, in three hours, but on foot, as most of the Passover pilgrims traveled, it took more than twice that long.

They set out early in the morning, the little group of apostles followed by a number of women, among them Mary of Magdala, Mary the mother of James and Joseph, Salome, and others. Mark says they used to accompany him on his tours and wait on him when he was in Galilee. Others of his Galilean followers had joined his general group, meaning to make the pilgrimage more or less in his society, joining his audience when he preached and trying to be near enough to hear what he might have to say.

As they approached the city and reached the point where the road to Bethany branched off toward the south, near a village called Bethphage, Jesus sent two of his disciples on ahead telling them that as they entered the next village they would find a colt that had never been ridden, tied. They were to untie it and bring it back to him. He went on,

"And if anybody says to you, 'Why are you doing that?' say, 'The Master needs it, and will send it back here directly.' "

Zechariah had long before predicted that the Messiah would enter the city "humble, and riding upon an ass, even upon a colt the foal of an ass" (Zechariah 9:9); the prophet called upon Jerusalem to welcome him with acclamation. It was with this prophecy in mind that Jesus had evidently taken measures while coming through Trans-Jordan, or while at Jericho, to have this animal in readiness for his use. The men in charge of the ass have their instructions, and his messengers have the expected answer. And all this is of great significance, for it means that in the Triumphal Entry into Jerusalem Jesus definitely assumed the role of the Messiah. That was what he had carefully planned. Where a man of the Western world would have stood up before an audience and said he was the Messiah, Jesus, in this highly Oriental fashion, even more unequivocally declared himself to be he, by riding into the city exactly as the prophet had foretold. It was his way of focusing attention upon himself and what he had to say to his nation, in his and their great crisis. It was no mere incident; it was a carefully planned declaration, for an immediate practical purpose. He is not simply fulfilling the prophecy; what is far more important for the biographer, he is doing it intentionally and on purpose

For, as was said earlier, what is most difficult in these last momentous days of his life is to look into the mind of Jesus and see his thoughts and purposes, and here is one of the utmost importance, which is unmistakably revealed to us by his acts. He meant his entry into the city, coupled with the occasion, and the acclamations of his followers, to be an announcement, unmistakable and unforgettable, that he is indeed God's Messiah, the Commissioner of the kingdom of heaven.

So when his messengers brought him the ass from the village street and threw their coats over it like an improvised saddlecloth, he mounted it, and rode it into the city. The people caught the idea and made his entering it a triumph. They threw their coats on the roadway before him, and brought straw from the fields to cover the muddy places in the road. Others brought branches and leaves to scatter before him. And before and behind him they shouted their joyful acclamations:

"God bless him!

"Blessed be he who comes in the Lord's name!

"Blessed be the reign of our father David which is coming!

"God bless him from on high."

The Jews bound for the Passover, as they neared Jerusalem, were used to singing favorite Psalms—122, 100, 48 and others—and to take up this chant was a natural thing for them as, their long tramp nearing its end, they began to see the towers and walls of the city coming into view. They were probably only half or three-quarters of an hour from the city, when Jesus mounted; it is only half an hour's walk from Bethany to Jerusalem.

So Jesus came to Jerusalem. By what gate he entered it, and found his way through its narrow crooked streets to the temple, we cannot say. The temple he visited has utterly disappeared; we can only trace some of its substructures under the pavement of the Haram area that forms the great courtyard of the Mosque of Omar, standing over the bare rock which was the threshing floor of Araunah the Jebusite and on which stood the high altar, the altar of burnt offering of Herod's temple. This splendid piece of Greek architecture, even then not quite finished, with its dazzling marbles and noble proportions filled the ordinary Jewish heart with pride.

Jesus looked it all over; he could pass through the Court of the Gentiles into the Court of the Women and beyond that into the Court of the Men of Israel. Beyond that lay the Court of the Priests, which he could not enter, and beyond that the curtain-covered holy place and sanctuary, the innermost shrine of the Jewish religion. The hour was late; it was a long walk from Jericho to Jerusalem, and the temple courts were beginning to be deserted. Jesus surveyed it all, no doubt planning what his course should be when he returned next morning. Then he and his disciples left the temple and the city and crossing the bed of the Kidron skirted the Mount of Olives, which rises two hundred feet above the city, and made their way to the security of Bethany, on its eastern slope, where they were to spend the nights.

CHAPTER XV

The Crisis at Jerusalem

For the last week of Jesus' life, the week spent in Jerusalem, we possess in the gospels a day-by-day account, and particularly that given by the Gospel of Mark in its simplicity and restraint rises to the very heights of heroic tragedy.

It was Monday morning, and they set out for the short walk, of perhaps half an hour, around the south shoulder of the Mount of Olives to Jerusalem. Jesus was hungry, a strange thing so early in the morning. Perhaps Bethany was so crowded with pilgrims that his party had been unable to get provisions. At all events he caught sight of a fig tree in full leaf, and when he reached it was disappointed at finding no figs on it, though it was not the time for figs. Yet if it had leaves, one might naturally expect at Passover time to find little unripe figs on it, or on the ground beneath it; they are often eaten, and even offered for sale. In his disappointment, he wished it might never bear any more fruit.

Reaching the city, he made his way at once into the courts of the temple, where in the Court of the Gentiles the temple money-changers had their places of business, changing the pilgrims' Roman money into the sacred currency the temple would accept. Here were also the sellers of the doves for sacrifice, as described in Leviticus 1:14. Jesus overturned the tables, and the dove-sellers' seats. As in the court of the Great Mosque in Damascus in modern times, porters carrying goods would make a short cut through the temple, and these Jesus ordered stopped. To the crowd that these high-handed proceedings attracted, he quoted the great oracle from the book of Isaiah,

"My house shall be called a house of prayer for all the nations," and yet if the Gentiles came there to pray, they would find their part of it full of petty business, in full swing. Instead of a house of prayer they had made it, as Jeremiah put it (7:11), a robbers' cave.

This was a bold attack in the name of religion upon the privileges and monopolies of the Sadducees, who occupied the priesthood and controlled the whole machinery of temple sacrifices and offerings. That was their monopoly, and they exploited it fully. In invading the Court of the Gentiles and interfering with the business done there, Jesus was making a frontal attack on the established order in Jerusalem and making a bold bid for a public hearing for his message.

He had begun his attack by his triumphal entry, thus announcing himself as a divinely commissioned leader; he continues it by this bold interference with established custom in temple—steps calculated to capture the attention of the Jewish public and the temple authorities. Jesus is seeking a decision, at Jerusalem. And he is doing it in the interests of just those little ones for whose welfare he was always so solicitous. The humble piety of the ordinary, everyday pilgrim ought not to be exploited to enrich the Sadducean aristocracy that controlled the temple. The priesthood had no business to make money out of the people's sacrifices; they were meant for the glory of God. And the Court of the Gentiles ought not to be a mere market place, but a house of prayer for all the nations, where even the heathen might find their way to God. On the barrier that bounded the Court of the Women at each gateway was a great inscription forbidding any alien to pass beyond it on pain of death; eighty years ago one of them was discovered almost intact. It was on suspicion that he had taken a Gentile named Trophimus past this barrier that Paul was mobbed and then arrested in this very court, a quarter of a century later. Jesus' interest extends even to the excluded Gentiles; even they should find in this court a place to pray, if the prophet was right! So Jesus' action was not mere drama, nor a mere challenge to the priestly proprietors of the temple; it was one more affirmation of rights contemporary Judaism denied. We have seen him speaking out for woman, for childhood, for the individual; here even the heathen is given his due.

All this quickly found its way to the high priests and scribes, the lords of the temple and its privileges. There was properly but one high priest, in Jesus' day appointed by the Roman governor of Judea. He was Caiaphas, who had been appointed some twelve years before by Pilate's predecessor, Valerius Gratus. His father-in-law Annas had been high priest for a short time not long before the appointment of Caiaphas, and still retained much of his previous influence and authority. These two are the "high priests" of the period, though perhaps other surviving ex-high priests are also meant in the gospels by the plural "high priests."

For more than two hundred years the Sadducees had been influential in Jewish religious life, and in Jesus' day they included the powerful priests and aristocrats—in short, the wealth and influence of Judea. They accepted only the Law of Moses as scripture, and rejected the Pharisaic doctrines of resurrection, together with the existence of angels and spirits. They had commercialized the temple worship, as indeed all temple worships were in that day commercialized, and conducted the worship of Judaism in ways acceptable to their Roman masters. To the religious condition of the people scattered through the country they gave little heed, demanding only that they steadily support the feasts and sacrifices at Jerusalem. The Pharisees were thus of little importance in Jerusalem, but they had their scribes there, and they participated in the deliberations of the Sanhedrin, the religious governing body of the Jews. But Jesus had already incurred the hostility of the Pharisees up in Galilee, and scribes from Jerusalem had been called in to examine into his proceedings. And now the Pharisees are more than ready to cooperate with the Sadducees in resenting what he did. They had long wanted to put an end to him and, with the cooperation of the Sadducees, began to see their desired goal in sight. But how to do it presented a serious problem, for his evident strength with the people insured his safety in his daytime visits to the temple, and at night he and his disciples went out of the city to Bethany, and spent the night there.

Next morning as they set out for Jerusalem again, Peter noticed that the fig tree which had disappointed Jesus the day before had withered up, and he pointed it out, characteristically explaining it by what Jesus had said of it. Jesus answered him with a striking saying about the power of faith, less with reference to the fig tree than to the prodigious task he was facing. He turned their thoughts from a withering fig tree to higher things. He had mountains to move in Jerusalem, but faith could do even that. But he would carry on his campaign in a spirit of forgiveness.

It was Tuesday, the third day of the Jewish week. Jesus and his group of followers, the disciples and others attracted by the hope of hearing him speak, walked about the temple. The Court of the Gentiles was an enormous platform, more than nine hundred feet wide and eleven hundred feet long. It was surrounded by magnificent colonnades, that on the south made up of four rows of lofty columns, those on the east, west and north being made up of three rows. The temple proper, a lofty group of buildings measuring about four hundred feet by five hundred, stood in this court toward the northern end. This stupendous structure was the material fortress of the rulers of the Jewish religion. It was the physical symbol of their pride and power. At the great festivals, the pious peasantry of all Palestine wandered about it with mingled awe and gratification. They felt it was Judaism's answer to the huge heathen structures, the temple of Artemis in Ephesus, the Serapeum in Alexandria, and the Capitol in Rome, the last two then the greatest buildings in the world.

It was in such a setting that a deputation of high priests, scribes and elders confronted Jesus, and boldly challenged his right to upset their established arrangements of money-changers and dove-sellers. It was not his teaching but his acts that they demanded an explanation of.

"What authority have you for doing as you do? And who gave you a right to do as you are doing?"

It was Jesus the man of action that had roused them, and brought this striking combination of Jewish authority together to confront him. For the scribes were a Pharisaic order, and the elders were members of the Sanhedrin, the council of seventy-one members, appointed from the leading priests, heads of prominent Sadducean families, and eminent Pharisaic scholars, or scribes, who formed the final court of appeal in Jewish matters in Judea. It was therefore a semiofficial body that now approached Jesus in his walk about the temple, and demanded his credentials.

He answered them without hesitation.

"Let me ask you one question, and if you answer me, I will tell you what authority I have for doing as I do. Was John's baptism from heaven, or from men? Answer me."

This question did not merely turn the tables upon them, it struck at the basis of their own inquiry. For his authority and John's came from the same source, the will of God.

Its immediate effect was to set them to arguing with one another. If they said it was from heaven, he would ask why they had not believed him. On the other hand, to say it was from men would offend the people, so many of whom believed John was really a prophet. They could only answer,

"We do not know."

This exposure of their spiritual bankruptcy was a stinging blow to their professed competence as settlers of all religious problems, and brought their onslaught upon him to an abrupt halt. He replied,

"Nor will I tell you what authority I have for doing as I do!"

With the Sanhedrin deputation still hovering near, he began to teach them and the throng that the encounter with them had collected about him, resuming his favorite method of teaching by parable.

From the times of Isaiah (Chapter 5) and from the Psalms, the Jews were familiar with the idea of Israel as God's vineyard, and Jesus talked of that vineyard.

"A man once planted a vineyard, and fenced it in and hewed out a wine vat and built a watch-tower, and he leased it to tenants, and left the neighborhood. At the proper time he sent a slave to the tenants to get from them a share of the vintage. And they took him and beat him and sent him back empty-handed. And again he sent another slave to them. And they beat him over the head and treated him shamefully. And he sent another, and him they killed; and so with many others, some they beat and some they killed.

"He still had one left to send; a dearly loved son. He sent him to them last of all, thinking, 'They will respect my son!' But the tenants said to one another, 'This is his heir! Come on, let us kill him, and the property will belong to us!' So they took him and killed him, and threw his body outside of the vineyard.

"What will the owner of the vineyard do? He will come back and put the tenants to death, and give the vineyard to others. Did you never read this passage of scripture—

"That stone which the builders rejected
Has become the corner-stone;
This came from the Lord,
And seems marvelous to us?"

The bearing of the parable's picture of the treatment the Jewish people had so often given their prophets was unmistakable, and its application to the attitude the temple authorities were taking toward him was only too apparent. The delegation wanted to arrest him, for they knew the illustration was aimed at them, but he was too strong with the people for them to risk it, and while the people might not have been able to protect him, the riot they would have made might have very unfavorable results with the Roman authorities, on whom the high priest depended for the tenure of his office. They withdrew from the attack, to plan some other stratagem.

The parable shows that Jesus' baptism experience of being in a special sense the Son of God still dominates his mind. He is warning the priestly crew against crowning the long Jewish record of doing violence to the prophets by the even more fearful crime of destroying himself, God's supreme and loftiest messenger.

The Old Testament oracle of the rejected cornerstone from Psalm 118:22, 23 describes a cut stone, neglected for some time by the builders of the temple, perhaps, but in the end found to be designed for the climax of the whole structure. The words meant by the Psalmist to describe the world's neglect of Israel are now applied to the rejection of the Messiah, the son in the story of the vineyard.

Matthew's account of this event carries us much further, and seems to reflect the days when Matthew was written, a few years after the culmination of the Jewish War of A.D. 66-70, and the terrible scenes attendant upon the fall of Jerusalem, in which tragedy Josephus says eleven hundred thousand people perished. The evangelist saw in the ruin of the city and the nation the awful penalty for its rejection of its Messiah. The kingdom of God was to be taken away from them and given to a people that would produce its proper fruit. And as for the stone mentioned in the Psalm, whoever fell on it would be shattered, but whoever it fell upon would be pulverized! By the year 80, it had fallen upon them. So the evangelist looking back over fifty years of swiftly moving events interpreted the cornerstone of Jesus' quotation.

The next group to try to entrap Jesus into confusion or blunders consisted of Pharisees and their Galilean allies the Herodians, or agents of Herod Antipas. They raised a well-worn question, that of paying tribute to the Roman emperor, which it was hardly possible to answer without giving serious offense to some important group in Judaism. The Zealots considered it wrong to pay it; the Pharisees, who cared only for their religious liberties, regarded it with indifference. The Pharisees approached him with apparent approval:

"Master, we know that you tell the truth regardless of the consequences, for you are not guided by personal considerations but teach the way of God with sincerity. Is it right to pay the poll tax to the emperor or not? Should we pay it, or refuse to pay it?"

Jesus detected their design, and said to them,

"Why do you put me to such a test? Bring me a denarius to look at."

They brought him one, a small silver coin about the size of our ten-cent piece, bearing on its face the profile portrait of the reigning emperor Tiberius, almost encircled by his name and title "Tiberius Caesar, son of the deified Augustus, (himself) Augustus." Jesus had seen many such coins, but for his own purpose he asked the men who brought it to him,

"Whose head and title is this?"

They told him,

"The emperor's."

Jesus said,

"Pay the emperor what belongs to the emperor, and pay God what belongs to God!"

They were astonished at his answer, for its boldness and decision. It leaned very much toward the side of the Pharisees, but he had coupled with it a strong assertion that God's demands were equally imperative. Certainly there was nothing of the revolutionary in his reply.

Now the Sadducees took up the debate. They did not believe in resurrection, a doctrine that had established itself in Judaism with the rise of the Pharisees in the second century before Christ, and came to him with a story designed to reduce it to absurdity, as they thought. It had to do with the old Mosaic law of levirate marriage, that is, the duty of a brother to take as his wife the widow of a deceased brother, if the brother had left no children, so much did the Hebrews value having posterity to carry on the family after they were gone. Of course with their easygoing attitude toward polygamy there was nothing to interfere with a surviving brother's carrying out this obligation, the children of such a marriage being theoretically those of the deceased.

The Sadducees told Jesus about a man who died, leaving no children. He was the eldest of seven brothers, and on his death the next eldest brother married his widow, and also died, leaving no children. So did all the rest of the seven brothers. The question was, in the resurrection, which one's wife will she be? The story reminds one a little of Sarah and her seven husbands in the Book of Tobit, which may have suggested it to the Sadducees.

Jesus replied that when people rise, there is no marrying or being married, but they live as the angels do in heaven, and reminded them of what God said to Moses in a famous passage in what we know as Exodus, "I am the God of Abraham, the God of Isaac, and the God of Jacob," clearly implying that he was still their God when he spoke to Moses, centuries after they had died, and that the relation of trust and dependence that had existed between them and God had not been interrupted by death. God, he said, was not the God of dead men, but of living. The story is also very significant as it shows Jesus' own belief in the future life. Jesus saw that the idea of the future life was involved in the soul's relation to God. If we can have communion with him, and come to trust and love him, we have entered upon a spiritual relationship which death cannot destroy. Modern Jewish scholars dismiss this argument as fanciful but it is far from being that. As St. Augustine said, probably quoting the second-century Odes of Solomon, "Join yourself to the eternal God, and you will be eternal."

In both these encounters, that with the Pharisees and that with the Sadducees, Jesus' answers had leaned toward the Pharisees' side, as compared with the Sadducees, and one of the scribes of the Pharisees felt that he was answering them well. So, not to test him, but with a sincere interest in his view of a vexed question, he put one to him.

"Which is the first of all the commands?"

Jesus gave the characteristic Jewish answer, quoting the Shema (Listen!), which served as the call to prayer in Jewish liturgy, and is still the cornerstone of Judaism:

"Listen, Israel! The Lord our God is one lord, and you must love the Lord your God with your whole heart, your whole soul, your whole mind, and your whole strength."

This was good Judaism. And he added,

"And this is the second: 'You must love your neighbor as you do yourself.' No other command is greater than these."

This second commandment was drawn from Leviticus 19:18, where it clearly refers to one's fellow-Jew, as the connection shows. The scribe was pleased with both answers, and strongly endorsed what Jesus had said.

"Really, Master, you have finely said that he stands alone, and there is none but he, and to love him with one's whole heart, one's whole understanding, and one's whole strength, and to love one's neighbor as one's self, is far more than all these burnt-offerings and sacrifices."

It was indeed an answer in line with what Amos and Hosea had said long before, and shows that Jesus was not seeking to quarrel with what was good in Judaism but welcomed it. He had already shown no hesitation in accepting what was accepted Pharisaic doctrine, in the matter of the poll tax and the resurrection, and that he could reach common ground with some Pharisees is clear enough from this last exchange. He was not without hope of winning the religious leaders of his people to his views, and had they consented to accept him, what an era of moral and religious leadership might have opened before them! The prophets had hoped for such a day.

Jesus was pleased at the scribe's response. He saw that the man had answered thoughtfully, and he said to him, "You are not far from the kingdom of God!"

It may not be without significance that Jesus in the gospels in quoting this classic item in Jewish liturgy invariably introduces the word "mind" or "understanding" into the series, as a fourth instrument for loving God. Jewish translators of the Hebrew (Deuteronomy 6:5) render "with all thy heart and with all thy soul and with all thy might," but Jesus' form of the command, as given in Matthew 22:37 reads "mind" for might, while Mark 12:30 and Luke 10:27, though in different orders, add "your whole mind." The scribe in agreeing with Jesus repeats the command after him, "with one's whole heart, one's whole understanding, and one's whole strength," and some modern Christian scholars translate Deuteronomy 6:5 "with all your mind, and all your heart and all your strength." But Dr. R. H. Charles, the scholarly archdeacon of Westminster, felt that Jesus had here made a positive and important advance upon the ancient form of the great command, adding intelligence to the great demand for zeal of the ancient Hebrew. In loving God, one did not need to close one's mind! Quite the opposite.

No one asked him any more questions, and he raised one himself.

"How can the scribes say that the Christ is a son of

David? David himself under the influence of the holy Spirit said,

" 'The Lord has said to my lord, Sit at my right hand, Until I put your enemies under your feet.'

David himself calls him lord, and how can he be his son?"

This saying accepts the Davidic authorship of the Psalms, or at least of Psalm 110, which was a general Jewish way of referring to them. The Jews thought loosely of the Law as the work of Moses, the Psalms as the work of David, and the Proverbs as that of Solomon. They were uninterested in literary authorship. This looseness of thinking marked their attitude toward measurements, distances, and chronology. Their genius lay in other fields than science or history. But understanding David to have written the Psalm, and his "lord" to be the Messiah, if the Messiah was to be a descendant of David, David as an Oriental could hardly call him lord and thus admit himself inferior to one of his own descendants.

The purpose of this is evidently to declare that the Messiah is far more than a mere descendant of David; he comes with a divine commission, not a mere royal descent. Jesus' point is that the Messiah is no mere political figure, important because he is of Davidic descent, but a great religious one, important because God has anointed him with the Spirit, and so great that God has destined for him a place at his own right hand.

The Son of David had of course become a Messianic title, with manifest political implications, which Jesus rejects. Yet notwithstanding this incident in the temple, which Matthew, Mark and Luke record, there are numerous cases where he is hailed as "Son of David" by enthusiastic groups or people in need of his help, and he had not refused the title. The genealogy at the beginning of Matthew by its title designates him as descended from David, and the genealogy there and the very different one in the third chapter of Luke trace his descent through David. A thousand years had passed since David's prime, and almost every Jew in Palestine must have had some Davidic blood; Jesus could hardly have escaped it. It must be clear that what he is here denying is not his own physical descent from David, but the use of that expression as an adequate description of the Messiah, who is far more than that title conveys. He is now definitely concerned to divest the title of its political color, which was not only misleading but dangerous, and bring out its loftier religious meaning, as the one to which the Psalm in question, messianically understood, really pointed.

The people who thronged the temple courts liked to hear him, and he took occasion to warn them against the pretensions of the Pharisees, their self-constituted religious leaders throughout the land.

"Beware of the scribes who like to go about in long robes, and to be saluted with respect in public places, and to have the front seats in the synagogues and the best places at dinners—men that eat up widows' houses, and to cover it up make long prayers! They will get a far heavier sentence!"

He had in mind the Pharisees who had made religion a profession, and posed conspicuously as its embodiments. It is the spiritual pride that had come to characterize them that he deplores and condemns.

Matthew presents this condemnation of the virtual leaders of Jewish religion in Chapter 23 in a detailed and extended form. Matthew wrote his gospel up in Syria fifty years later, at a time and place in which Jewish and Christian ways of life were in vigorous conflict. His account of Jesus' arraignment of the Pharisees has no doubt taken on stronger colors in the half-century of life-and-death struggle that has intervened. Yet there is still much truth in the stern picture and basically it must reflect the mind of Jesus. For Pharisaism in its zeal for the Jewish religion had come to identify it with the preservation of the Jewish people in isolation from all other groups. This attitude exalted sheer differentness into a major virtue, since it buttressed their preservation as a distinct people. Indeed, it made it a dogma of religion, at the very opposite pole from Christianity, which was finding its way to the very contrary affirmation, "Unless a grain of wheat falls on the ground and dies, it remains just one grain. But if it dies, it yields a great harvest"—John 12:24. This was precisely what Pharisaism did not believe.

Jesus contrasts the good things they tell men to do with their own pride, complacency and ostentation. Pharisees wore wide scripture texts as charms, and liked to be called Rabbi—"my master." Jesus would have people use no such vain titles, for the greatest of them must be their servant, for whoever exalts himself will be humbled, and whoever humbles himself will be exalted.

A deeper fault with Pharisaism lay in the fact that its refinements of the Law, devised to protect it from any possible violation, had hedged it about with such frivolous detail that the poor and ignorant people of the land could not observe it, and were by that very fact cut off from the comfort and support of religion. Pharisaism had made religion an aristocratic privilege. We shall find Jesus returning to this matter in the last and greatest of his parables, the Last Judgment. They were locking the doors of the kingdom of heaven in men's faces; they would neither go in themselves nor let those go in that wanted to do so. They were infinitely scrupulous about tithing, computing the required tenth upon the very smallest articles of food, the flavorings and extracts used in cooking, for fear they might unwittingly break the law, yet they left undone the far greater matters, justice, mercy and faith. Why, as we have seen, a Pharisee spying a gnat in his drink would go to all the trouble of straining whatever was in his cup, to avoid breaking the law of Leviticus 11:23, 43 against eating the tiniest winged insect, and yet go out and, in comparison, swallow a camel!

Another fatal flaw in Pharisaism as Jesus saw it was its externalizing of religion. It was all so detailed and defined that one's attention was absorbed in externals, the outside of the dish, and the heart and essence of the religious life, the attitude of spirit, was forgotten and neglected. But that was what mattered most; in fact, it was everything.

Once a man's heart was right, and he had made God's will his own, the externals and details would take care of themselves.

Matthew's terrible statement, that all the righteous blood shed on earth from the blood of Abel to their own day will come upon their heads, shows the influence of the fall of Jerusalem in A.D. 70, when such tremendous numbers of Jews perished in the siege and capture of the city. In that frightful catastrophe Christians saw the punishment of Jerusalem for rejecting Jesus and putting him to death. Certainly they had tried again and again to silence him in Galilee.

The discourse in Matthew reaches its climax in the touching lament over Jerusalem.

In the Court of the Women, raised a number of steps above the floor level of the great Court of the Gentiles, was located the treasury with a row of trumpet-shaped receptacles for gifts, and many people of wealth were putting in the gifts they had brought to Jerusalem, and changed at the tables of the money-changers in the Court of the Gentiles into coinage acceptable by the temple. It was a conspicuous act of piety, and such ostentation in benevolence had offended Jesus before, and led him to denounce those hypocritical givers who, as it were, had a trumpet sounded before them, in the synagogue or in the street, to call attention to their giving—that is, gave as conspicuously as possible. Some Pharisees denounced such practices, but there are such people in every age.

What especially caught Jesus' attention, however, was

the gift of a poor woman, evidently a widow, who shyly dropped two little copper coins into the mouth of one of the receptacles. Jesus was near enough to see the smallness of her contribution, and felt the relative greatness of her sacrifice. He called his disciples to him and said to them,

"I tell you, this poor widow has put in more than all these others who have been putting money into the treasury! For they gave of what they had to spare, but she in her want has put in everything she possessed—all she had to live on!"

These four verses about the Widow's Mite form the longest passage in Mark that does not reappear in Matthew, and for the obvious reason that Matthew makes so much of Jesus' denunciation of public giving that his praise of the woman's public act probably seemed to the evangelist out of line with his great hyperbole that when you give to charity you must not let your left hand know what your right hand is doing.

As they left the temple that afternoon, one of the disciples, overwhelmed with the massive splendor of the great fabric, said to him,

"Look, Master! What wonderful stones and buildings!"

He might well exclaim, no matter how many times he may have seen them before. Much of the east side of the foundation wall is still there to awe the modern visitor, with blocks of stone two and a half feet thick and twenty-six, sometimes twenty-seven and a half, feet long, perhaps hewn and put in place in the days of Solomon. Above them rose the colonnade that surrounded the great court, with its hundreds of marble columns, while the sanctuary itself rose, it is said, to a height of a hundred and fifty feet above the floor of the great court. This floor in turn was high above the Kidron Valley that ran along the east side of the temple wall, which was also the east wall of the city.

Jesus said to him,

"Do you see these great buildings? Not one stone shall be left here upon another that shall not be torn down!"

They left the temple in a somber mood, crossed the Kidron Valley and went up on the Mount of Olives, which faced the temple hill across the little valley and towered above it. From it then as now there was a fine view of the city, then of course at the height of its splendor. His four fishermen disciples, the men he had called first from their boats on the Sea of Galilee, must have been greatly struck by his dire prediction, and they drew him aside.

"Tell us," they said, "when this is to happen and what the sign will be when it is all just going to be carried out."

Standing on the verge of eternity that spring afternoon in Jerusalem, Jesus saw mankind's future immensely foreshortened. We call it apocalyptic. But to us today Macaulay's fantasy of the New Zealander ages hence dreaming among the ruins of St. Paul's no longer seems amusing or remote. We know how near it came in 1941 to coming terribly true; the cloisters of Westminster did not escape destruction. And to one great physicist it no longer seems impossible that the explosive ingenuity of man may blow up not just London or New York but the whole world, if the right chain reaction is hit upon. We ourselves may be living closer to actual apocalyptic realization than people have ever lived before, if by apocalyptic is meant the end of our world and of human life as we know it.

To Jesus it may well have seemed that Roman and Jewish currents were moving toward inevitable catastrophe. The Zealots and nationalistic revolutionaries on the one side, and the ruthless and rigid policies of the Roman empire on the other, with callous and unprincipled Roman governors and Jewish high priests to spark the explosion, promised eventual disaster for city and nation, unless the kingdom of heaven should win such support that his people would turn to living as men belonging to another world. But his experience in Jerusalem has made him feel that this is not to be, and the explosion of which he has seen so many signs about him must occur. Peering into the future, he envisaged strange shapes of things to come. Nation would rise against nation, and kingdom against kingdom; there would be earthquakes here and there, there would be famines. These would be only the beginnings of the sufferings. But when they saw these things happening, they might know that the Son of Man was at hand.

A sense of great immediacy possessed him. "I tell you," he went on, "these things will all happen before the present age passes away. Earth and sky will pass away, but my words will never pass away. But about that day or hour no one knows, not even the angels in heaven, nor the Son, only the Father. You must look out and be on the alert, for you do not know when it will be time; just as a man when he leaves home to go on a journey, and puts his slaves in charge, each with his duties, gives orders to the watchman to keep watch. So you must be on the watch, for you do not know when the master of the house is coming—in the evening or at midnight or toward daybreak or early in the morning—for fear he should come unexpectedly, and find you asleep! And what I am telling you I mean for all— Be on the watch!"

These words came later to be interwoven with reflections of the experiences of the early believers under persecution and betrayal, during the next forty years, mixed with their flight from the doomed city toward the year 70, and the dreadful misery it involved. Particularly, the reference to the "dreadful desecration," which in Daniel 9:27 meant the pagan altar set up on the great altar in Jerusalem by the king of Syria, probably reflects some Roman act of temple desecration offensive to Jewish piety on the eve of the Jewish War of A.D. 66-70. The flight of the Judean Christians into the hills was to escape the siege of the city which ensued, and all its horrors. A wealth of historical references from the next forty years can easily be distinguished in this thirteenth chapter of Mark.

This does not alter the fact that Jesus himself used this bold apocalyptic phraseology, about coming on the clouds of heaven and sitting at the right hand of power, as the vehicle for his own conviction of the ultimate dramatic and overwhelming triumph of the kingdom of God on earth. His rhetoric knew nothing of the restraint characteristic of the Greek genius; the Hebrew lay in just the other direction, and it was he who carried this Hebrew genius of expression to its greatest heights. And nowhere more than in his apocalyptic pictures of the Messianic future. But as a matter of fact, this was the basis of the whole apocalyptic language, which Western minds took far too literally, and was in every case highly figurative, being one of the ways Hebrew religious teachers took to gain contemporary human attention. There is no doubt that more matter-of-fact minds unfamiliar with Oriental modes of speech have created difficulties for themselves in trying to interpret literally the apocalyptic school, and Jesus, who used so much of its vocabulary, and indeed gave it its highest expression.

In those momentous hours on the Mount of Olives, as Jesus sat talking to his disciples, as Matthew records it, his teaching in parables reached its climax in a series of three stories.

"The kingdom of heaven," he began, "will be like ten bridesmaids, who took their lamps and went out to meet the bridegroom." Everyone remembers the inimitable story. Five were wise, and took extra oil for the tiny lamps they carried, but five were foolish and did not. Everyone knows their sad story; they were shut out of the wedding banquet.

Another is the parable of the talents, the story of a man who entrusted large sums of money to his slaves, five thousand dollars to one, two thousand to another and one thousand to a third. The first and second went immediately to work, going into business with this capital, and when long afterward he came back, and inquired about what they had done, they reported handsome gains. But the third man distrusted his master, and buried his money in the ground, to keep it safe until his return. This cautious procedure displeased his master very much; it was no way to deal with the gifts of life.

The third, in some ways the grandest of all the parables, is that of the Last Judgment. The point of it is, why some were approved and put on the king's right hand, and some were disapproved and put on his left, which is what everybody wants to know about the Last Judgment. Jesus made it perfectly plain and unanswerable. He said that when they asked the king, "Lord, when did we see you hungry or thirsty, or a stranger, or in need of clothes, or sick, or in prison, and did not wait upon you?" he would reply, "In so far as you failed to do it for one of these people who are humblest, you failed to do it for me!"

This way of putting our duties to our fellow-men has never since been equaled. And it suddenly dawns upon you, as it must have dawned upon them, that the point of the story is not this colossal phantasmagoria of the universal judgment of all mankind but the moral demand that will inevitably be the basis of such a judgment.

And this was just the flaw Jesus found so unendurable in Pharisaism. Claiming to possess the monopoly of the grace and mercy of God, the Pharisees made its terms impossible for those who were least—the poor, unprivileged part of the population, the "people of the land," who could not begin to keep up with the requirements the Pharisees had set up for religion. They had definitely refused to do it for those who were least, and this Jesus recognized as the one thing that was unpardonable in the custodians of religion.

CHAPTER XVI

The Transformation of the Passover

Meantime, across the valley in the temple, the high priests and scribes, that is, Sadducees and Pharisees, deeply incensed at what he had done and said, were putting their heads together in a plot to arrest him by stealth and have him put out of the way. The Sadducees he had offended by his violent clearing out of the commercialism of the Court of the Gentiles. The Pharisees had been looking for a way to get rid of him ever since he had begun to preach in Galilee. This was a coalition so strong as to be irresistible, and yet they were not ready to provoke a riot by arresting him boldly in the temple in broad daylight. In fact, they meant to do nothing until the feast was over, and the great crowds of people had left the city for their homes.

After the conversation about the fall of the city, and Jesus' sad farewell to Jerusalem, Jesus and his disciples made their way around the shoulder of the Mount of Olives to Bethany, where he seems to have been lodging at the house of Simon the leper, as Mark calls him. Probably he was one of the men Jesus had cured; at any rate Mark regarded that as a sufficient identification of him. As they sat at supper, a woman who knew that he was there came in with an alabaster flask of expensive perfume, and breaking it poured the perfume upon his head. Anointing the head of a guest with fragrant oil was a part of Hebrew courtesy—

"Thou anointest my head with oil,
My cup runneth over"—

though it was really the part of the host to provide such attentions (Luke 7:46). Some of the other guests, who were mostly his disciples, and poor men, were indignant at such extravagance. They exclaimed that it was wasteful, for the perfume might have been sold for a large sum of money and the money given to the poor. They loudly condemned the woman for wasting it.

Jesus, however, stood up for her. He saw in her action its emotional value; it showed how much she thought of him and his work. It was probably the most valuable thing she possessed, and she had lavished it upon giving him a moment's pleasure and doing him honor. Thoughts of his own great peril too colored his attitude.

"Let her alone," he told them. "Why do you bother her? It is a fine thing that she has done to me. You always have the poor among you, and whenever you please you can do for them, but you will not always have me. She has done all she could; she has perfumed my body in preparation for my burial!" The prospect of his early death had never been far from his thoughts, from the time he left Galilee for the journey to the festival. Now he went on to say,

"I tell you, wherever the good news is preached all over

the world, what she has done will also be told, in memory of her."

Jesus himself was not counting the cost, and he could understand the mood of the woman, who was ready to give her best.

The idea of Montefiore (*The Synoptic Gospels*, I, 318) that he can have had no presentiments, nor expressed any, as no one had threatened him, and there was really nothing to be afraid of, is negatived by the whole narrative of Mark, and most of all by the dreadful sequel. Those were times of violence and bloodshed. There was the fate of John the Baptist, a few months before, and not so many months later that of Stephen, right there in Jerusalem, shows what the Jewish temper there was, almost in the very days of Jesus. And not many years after, Paul was five times given the traditional thirty-nine stripes, by synagogue authorities, in Palestine or Asia Minor, and narrowly escaped death at Damascus not long after the death of Jesus. A few years later John's brother James was put to death by Herod Agrippa, evidently at the instance of the Jews, and Peter had a narrow escape. But eventually Paul, Peter and John were all killed. The penalty for blasphemy, the charge made against Jesus, was death by stoning (Lev. 24:16), and the Jews were collectively responsible, under that law, for executing the sentence with their own hands. Twenty years later, Paul was stoned and left for dead by a Jewish body at Lystra, in Asia Minor, and Jesus' brother James, Josephus says, was stoned to death by the Jews at Jerusalem in A.D. 62, at the instance of the high priest Annas, the son of the Annas of the gospel story.

Meantime Judas felt that the time had come for him to act. What can have animated him, whether he had always been a traitor at heart, looking for a chance to make something for himself out of Jesus' friendship, or whether he had a mad confidence that an actual attack upon Jesus would force his hand and stir him to some supernatural demonstration that would put him and his apostles in control of things, we cannot say. At any rate he got in touch with the high priests, and undertook to betray Jesus' whereabouts to them at a given time, so that they could seize him with nobody about to interfere. Perhaps the incident at Simon's house in Bethany precipitated his action. From this point on, at any rate, he was watching for his chance.

Jesus was very anxious to eat the Passover supper with his disciples, and on Thursday morning, when his disciples asked him where he wished them to make their preparations for it, he told two of them—Luke says Peter and John —to go into Jerusalem, where they would meet a man carrying a pitcher of water. They should follow him, and in the house that he entered they should say to the man of the house,

"The Master says, where is my room, where I can eat the Passover supper with my disciples?"

The man would show them a large room upstairs, furnished and ready, and in it the disciples were to make the necessary preparations.

It is clear that Jesus had made these arrangements in advance, even to the finding of the house by following the man with the pitcher, just as he had prearranged to have the animal for him to ride into the city waiting at a convenient place when he was approaching Jerusalem. He now felt his personal peril so keenly that he was resolved to take every precaution so as not to be interrupted and arrested before the Passover supper, upon which he laid so much stress, was eaten.

Mark dates this conversation "on the first day of the festival of Unleavened Bread, when it was customary to kill the Passover lamb," and the first day, on which the lamb was killed, did not begin until sunset. Some scholars object that the lamb was killed on the second day, that is, after sunset or at dusk on Thursday, which the Jews characteristically considered part of the next day. But Mark is writing Greek, not Aramaic, and very reasonably counts days as we do, so as to be intelligible to his readers. According to the provision in Exodus 12:6, and Leviticus 23:5, 6, it is to be done "between the two evenings," which translators from Tyndale down have taken as: about even, at even, in the evening, between sunset and dark, at twilight —not, as Montefiore renders it, "toward sunset." Even the effort made in Deuteronomy 16 to articulate the Passover with the festival of Unleavened Bread leaves the matter uncertain, fixing the time of sacrificing the Passover as in the evening, at sunset, of the first day (verses 4 and 6).

But what the Jews called the evening of the first day we would call the evening before the first day, or the "eve" of the first day. As the Jews reckoned days, the evening of Thursday the thirteenth of Nisan would be the fourteenth, and it was then that the lamb was killed. Modern Jews understand the meaning to be that. As the creation story shows, the Jews counted evening and morning as making the day, so what we call the evening of the thirteenth they would call the evening of the fourteenth, their "day" running from sunset to sunset. But Mark is writing for Greeks who knew nothing of these quaint ways of speech, and found them as difficult as we do.

The festival of Unleavened Bread, a sort of Hebrew spring housecleaning festival, ushered in by the Passover sacrifice and supper, began in what we would call the evening of the thirteenth of Nisan, but the Jews called the fourteenth and counted as the first day of the festival. The disciples went into the city, found the man with the water pitcher, as Jesus had described him, and followed him to the house where the man of the house, evidently communicated with before by Jesus, received them and provided what they needed for the supper.

The usual Passover supper was punctuated with the four cups of red wine and water, the first of which was first blessed and then drunk or tasted. Then they all washed their hands (they ate of course with their fingers) and a prayer was offered, or repeated. The second cup was then drunk, and the origin of the festival was explained by the head of the household. The first part of the "Hallel" ("Praise!"), Psalms 113 and 114, was then sung. The food consisted of the roasted lamb and the unleavened bread, not a loaf to slice, as with us, but a smaller, flattish cake of bread, which would be broken with the fingers. A sauce of dates, raisins and vinegar was probably at hand in a dish, into which the broken pieces of bread or the bitter herbs might be dipped. Over the third cup a thanksgiving was uttered, and after the fourth, the rest of the Hallel, Psalms 115 to 118, was sung. This was the "hymn" the singing of which is mentioned in the gospels as concluding the supper.

In the evening Jesus and the rest of the disciples left Bethany, where he had probably spent every night this far, and took the short walk around the shoulder of the Mount of Olives, across the Kidron to the city. He, or they, if Peter and John had rejoined them, knew the way to the house, and there they took their places about the table.

He had looked forward with the keenest anticipation to eating this Passover with them, and now took his place at the table with something like a sigh of relief. His fears that he would not be able to celebrate the Passover with them had not been realized, but throughout the meal he was deeply preoccupied with presentiments of his approaching death. He showed his feeling in his first words:

"How greatly I have desired to eat this Passover supper with you before I suffer!" For some reason he had been intensely anxious to have them all about him on this one more occasion. Presently he touched the subject again.

"I tell you, one of you is going to betray me—one who is eating with me!"

These terrible words naturally hurt them deeply, and they said to him reproachfully, one after another,

"Can it be I?"

The fact that they were eating with him should have

insured their absolute loyalty, but he goes on to say it is to
be one who is dipping his morsel of bread or vegetables in
the same dish with him, meaning no doubt the dish of
sauce that served the whole table.

"It is one of the twelve, who is dipping his bread in the
same dish with me. For the Son of Man is indeed to go
away as the scriptures say of him, but alas for the man by
whom the Son of Man is betrayed! It would have been
better for that man if he had never been born!"

With this terrible warning he sought to restrain any of
them who might be planning to betray him. The scripture
referred to was Isaiah's prophecy about the Suffering Servant of Jehovah (Isaiah 53). Isaiah's pictures had been in
Jesus' mind certainly ever since his reading of Isaiah 61 in
the synagogue at Nazareth.

As the supper progressed, he took one of the round cakes
of bread, and gave thanks over it, then breaking it in pieces
he passed them around among them.

"Take this," he said. "It is my body, which takes your
place. Do this in memory of me!"

In these solemn words he was clearly taking leave of
them and of this world. He was also commanding them
henceforth to make this supper a memorial to him, which
should perpetuate his memory and his message. We now
begin to understand why he had been so much concerned
to live to celebrate the Passover with them, and why he
had taken such precautions so that nothing might interfere
with his plan, and why he had shown such great relief
when they all sat down to supper. He proposed to make

this supper a great and most significant occasion, for it was
to be the vehicle for perpetuating his work and his memory. When he first chose the twelve to be an inner circle
and receive his private teaching, he had had Isaiah's example in mind, when he proposed "to seal the teaching in
the hearts of his disciples." Jesus now, with the intensifica-
tion of his danger and the conviction that his time was
short and his work done, seized upon this supper, and made
it for his disciples his memorial. The plain fact that it has
proved so must not blind us to the fact that that is what he
meant it to be.

He also meant it to weld them into a new society, based
upon their assurance that his death was not the end of his
work but the climax of it, as a great sacrifice to God on
men's behalf, which solemnized a new covenant between
God and men. His further words and actions, as Paul
records them some twenty years later, and Mark does
twenty years later still, confirm all this, and make the
occasion in effect the founding of the Christian church.

The time for the fourth and final cup had come. He
took it and gave thanks and gave it to them, and they all
drank from it. He said to them,

"This is my blood which ratifies the new agreement, and
is to be poured out for many people. Whenever you drink
it, do so in memory of me. I tell you I will never drink the
product of the vine again till the day when I shall drink
the new wine in the kingdom of God."

Paul saw in this deeply moving scene the institution of
the Christian fellowship, and declared that every time

believers ate this bread and drank from this cup they proclaimed Jesus' death. It is very probable that Paul's knowledge of these events was drawn from the oral gospel of the primitive church, to which he occasionally refers and which had nothing to do with our written gospels or their immediate sources.

After they had all drunk from the final cup of the Passover supper, and he had told them what it would mean to them in after years, they sang the usual hymn, the second part of the Hallel, Psalms 115 to 118, beginning,

> "Not unto us, O Lord, not unto us,
>   But to thy name give honor,"

and ending,

> "Give thanks to the Lord, for he is good,
>   For his kindness is everlasting."

Then they left the upper room, and found their way down the street to the gates and out of the city. But Jesus had had his wish, to eat that Passover with his closest, chosen friends, and he had done it in such a way as to stamp some things indelibly upon their memories. For now whatever happened to him, and he felt his danger was very near and very great, the Passover would always remind them, and all his followers after them, of him and his sacrifice, as he now knew it to be. Paul, who wrote his account of it, quite incidentally, in his first letter to the Corinthians only twenty-five years after, already understood that he had said to them, of eating the bread, "Do this in memory of me"; and of drinking the wine, "Whenever you drink it, do so in memory of me." Even without these particular injunctions to make it his memorial—as Mark gives it, "Take this; it is my body! . . . This is my blood, which ratifies the agreement (the covenant, or testament), and is to be poured out for many people"—it must have associated him forever with the supper in the minds of the twelve. He had seen in the supper, the great festival of Judaism, a means of perpetuating his fellowship and the memory of his sacrifice, and uniting the two. This must have been why he had been so eager and solicitous about celebrating the supper with them. As he had, when first conscious of personal danger up in Galilee, followed Isaiah's example of forming an inner circle of close disciples, who might carry on his work if he were taken away, so now again, when the danger is so close at hand, he takes a final step to cement and perpetuate that fellowship. For them at least and their followers, he will make the Passover supper his memorial, their Lord's Supper.

Jesus lived in a nonliterary world. The Hebrew people about him had given up writing books; they felt that in their scriptures all the books they needed had been written. He did not think in terms of biographies or gospels, but in terms of action and symbol. Where other men would write a will, or a farewell address, he performed an act, and charged them with its perpetuation. No wonder it still moves countless hearts to tears.

CHAPTER XVII

Gethsemane and the Trial

From the upstairs room in Jerusalem they went out of the city and up the Mount of Olives, on their way home to Bethany. Jesus was still downcast and apprehensive. He talked to them as they went.

"You will all desert me," he said. "For the scriptures say, 'I will strike the shepherd, and the sheep will be scattered.' But after I am raised to life again I will go back to Galilee before you."

It was evident that he was now convinced that his death was very near, but, as Hosea had said, God would raise him up, to rejoin them at some rendezvous in Galilee. Peter, however, stoutly demurred.

"Even if they all desert you," said he boldly, "I will not!"

But Jesus said to him,

"I tell you, this very night, before the cock crows twice, you yourself will disown me three times!"

But he persisted vehemently,

"If I have to die with you, I will never disown you!"

All of them said the same thing; they would never disown him.

It was a mild spring night, with a full moon, and Jesus

was inwardly too disturbed to go on to Bethany to bed. As they came to a garden called Gethsemane, he suggested that they should all sit down while he went further into the grove to pray. He took Peter, James and John along with him, and when they had gained a little privacy, he began to show the full measure of distress that had come over him. The presentiments and apprehensions that had haunted him all through the supper now swept over him with redoubled force and almost overwhelmed him. He was no Stoic; he tasted the depth of human experience of the dread and pain of death. He must be alone with this fearful experience; in their crowded lodgings at Bethany he could not hope to find the privacy he must have, for a little while. And yet he wanted his three companions close at hand. He said to them,

"My heart is almost breaking! You must stay here and keep watch."

He went a little further into the depths of the garden, but not out of earshot. There he threw himself on the ground and prayed that if it was possible he might be spared the hour of trial. They could hear his broken ejaculations.

"Father!" he pleaded, "anything is possible for you! Take this cup away from me!" And then after an interval, "Yet not what I please but what you do!"

They were too tired to keep awake long, however, and soon went to sleep. After a while he came back to where he had left them, and found them all asleep. But he wanted them awake, either as sentries or as possible company in his extremity.

"Simon," he called, "are you asleep? Weren't you able to watch for one hour? You must all watch, and pray that *you* may not be subjected to trial!" And yet he knew how tired they were, and added,

"One's spirit is eager, but human nature is weak."

Again he left them and returned to his painful vigil, praying again in the same words. He was gone some time, for when he came back to them they were all asleep again, for they simply could not keep their eyes open. Again he charged them to keep awake and watch, for he knew what a risk he was taking; this was the first night he had been out of doors, near the city, instead of safe in crowded Bethany. They did not know what to say to him.

When he came back to them the third time, he said to them,

"Are you still sleeping and taking your rest? Enough of this! The time is up! See, the Son of Man is betrayed into the hands of wicked men. Get up, let us be going! Look, here comes my betrayer!"

For just at that moment, while he was speaking, Judas came up with a crowd of men with swords and clubs, from the temple authorities, to arrest him.

We must not hastily blame the Jewish people for what ensued; a great many of them were really on his side, if they could have been fairly counted. It was the dominant crowd, the Rome-appointed high priest and his agents who controlled Jerusalem, who now went into action. (Pilate's predecessor had dismissed and replaced four high priests in rapid succession.) Judas had slipped away after the supper to inform the temple people, or perhaps he had waited until Jesus went into this particular garden on the slope of the Mount of Olives, and hurried down across the Kidron to some priest's office where he could call out the necessary guard. Some people have thought Judas was perhaps not so bad as he seems; that he may have believed in Jesus but felt he was not taking the bold line he should have taken, and headed a revolution against the priests and the governor; certainly afterward when he realized the consequences of his action, Matthew says he repented bitterly of what he had done and came back to the Sanhedrin authorities to say so and return the money they had paid him, and then went off and hung himself.

Judas had told them that he would walk right up to Jesus and kiss him, to show them which one to arrest. Men frequently greeted their friends with a kiss. He did so affectionately, saying, "Master!" so that there might be no mistake. The posse closed around Jesus and seized him. The disciples seem to have offered no resistance. A bystander friendly to Jesus, who had evidently followed the group of men brought by Judas, drew his sword and wounded the slave of the high priest, who was perhaps the leader of the crew.

Jesus uttered a brief protest.

"Have you come out to arrest me with swords and clubs, as though I were a robber? I have been among you day after day in the temple, teaching, and you never seized me. But let the scriptures be fulfilled!"

He was alluding to the words in Isaiah (53:6-9 and 12) about the Suffering Servant of Jehovah, with whom, as we have seen, he had before identified himself:

> "When he was oppressed, he humbled himself,
> And opened not his mouth;
> Like a sheep that is led to the slaughter, . . .
> He opened not his mouth."

In the confusion that followed, the disciples made their escape, though Peter put in an appearance in the court-yard of the high priest's house later in the night. The high priest's crew tried to hold everybody they could lay their hands on. The story in Mark of a young man with just a linen cloth around him, who only escaped by slipping out of it when the posse tried to hold him, is told to show that they were picking up everybody found near Jesus. There is a similar incident in the Greek papyri of a man's escaping arrest by the very same device.

So Jesus was left alone with his captors, who took him down across the Kidron into the sleeping city, to the house of Caiaphas the high priest. The high priest's palace was probably located in the southwestern quarter of the city, and the houses of the priestly aristocracy were in the same general neighborhood, so that they could be readily reached, although it must have been in the small hours after midnight.

The high priest and his household were roused from

sleep with the news that Jesus had been taken, and as soon as they could be reached and summoned the high priests, elders and scribes were got together, the three groups that formed the Sanhedrin, the official council of the Jews. By "high priests" the gospel story means the present and past high priests; the scribes, as we have seen, were a Pharisaic minority, though as far as Jesus was concerned they were in agreement with the Sadducean priests and householders.

Peter, who had slunk along at a safe distance, had the nerve to work his way into the open courtyard about which the high priest's residence was built. In the chill of early morning, the waiting guards had made a fire out there to keep themselves warm, and Peter edged up to it and warmed himself.

Meantime, in the inner chambers of the high priest's palace, that official and his full council were trying to find a charge on which they could make a claim to the governor that Jesus should be executed. Under their own law any charge had to be supported by at least two witnesses, and they could find nothing serious enough to bring against him before the Roman governor which could be supported by more than one witness. One man said he had heard Jesus say he would tear down their sanctuary built by men's hands and in three days build another made without hands—perhaps an allusion to his predictions of his resurrection. But nobody could be found to corroborate this.

The high priest finally got up, moved dramatically forward into the center of the gathering and, seeking to provoke Jesus into incriminating himself, said to him

"Have you no answer to make? What about their evidence against you?"

Jesus made no reply. He scorned to answer the governor's puppet, who thus hypocritically sought to challenge him.

The high priest made one more frantic effort.

"Are you the Christ, the Son of the Blessed One?" The Sadducees were very reluctant to utter the name of God; the First Book of Maccabees, a Sadducean book written a century earlier, never mentions the name of God. But with this question the high priest gave Jesus the opportunity to utter his great conviction, and he did not hesitate to reply.

"I am! and you will all see the Son of Man seated at the right hand of the Almighty, and coming in the clouds of the sky!"

This startling assertion gave the high priest all he wanted. He was sure he could get a conviction from the governor on this statement, but in a great pretense of horror and sorrow at such blasphemous words, he tore his clothes, oriental-fashion, and cried out to the council,

"What do we want of witnesses now? Did you hear his blasphemy? What is your decision?"

Thus put, the question was unanimously carried and the council condemned him to death. Yet Jewish scholars say that to claim to be Messiah was no crime in Jewish law, and think it more likely he was condemned for planning to destroy the temple, the charge on which the testimony did not agree, but which may have arisen from what he said about the certainty of its future destruction, as recorded in Mark 13:2. It seems more reasonable to conclude that the decisive charge was the one Mark gives, to which Jesus pleads guilty, as they put it—which was essentially, as they viewed it, blasphemy. It was also one they could lay before the governor, since it would seem to him to mean that Jesus meant to make himself king.

The malignity of his captors manifested itself in the usual indignities an ancient prisoner might expect, being spit upon, and also blindfolded, and struck, and asked if he was a prophet to tell who had hit him. Matthew brings this fact out, while Mark leaves it to the understanding of the reader. The guards to whom he was now returned also cuffed him as they took him away. His silence and composure under all these insults later reminded his followers of the words of Isaiah about the Suffering Servant (53:7); "He opened not his mouth."

Outside in the courtyard, meanwhile, Peter was still hanging around, waiting to see what the council was going to do with Jesus. To this extent Peter was making good on his loud protestations that he would never forsake Jesus, no matter what the others did. But he was unequal to the demands his presence there was to make upon him. One of the high priest's maids happened to come up, and seeing Peter warming himself took a second look at him, and said, perhaps teasingly at first,

"You were with this Jesus of Nazareth too!"

Now this was Peter's great opportunity to brave his Master's peril and share his probable fate. But he did not stop to think, but under the strong instinct of self-preservation took the safer course. He denied it, and said to her,

"I don't know or understand what you mean."

Then he left the fire and went out into the gateway; perhaps he was thinking about leaving the place altogether, since it was beginning to look dangerous to stay around the palace. But the irrepressible girl caught sight of him out there, and seeing she had annoyed him started in again.

"This fellow is one of them," she proudly informed the bystanders.

Peter denied it again. But after a little while, they said to Peter,

"You certainly are one of them, for you're a Galilean!"

They had detected a Galilean tone in his speech. He was by now getting concerned, and began to swear with the strongest oaths he could think of, that he was nothing of the kind.

"I do not know this man you are talking about!" he declared.

But at that moment a cock crowed the second time, and Peter suddenly remembered what Jesus had said to him at the supper the night before: "Before the cock crows twice, you will disown me three times!" Sorrow for the loss of his Master, and the disappointment of all his high hopes, and most of all the revelation of the poor stuff of his own character, overwhelmed him, and he broke down and cried aloud.

This famous story of Peter's denials can only have come

through Peter himself. No one else would have known it, in the first place, and if anyone else had known it, to have gone about telling it on poor Peter would have been a mean and most unchristian part to play. But imagine Peter years later before the Roman congregation, telling his own great failure, his crime against his Master and his agonized repentance. Who could have heard such a confession unmoved? It was precisely the fact that it came from Peter's own lips that gave it its moving power. And it was from the sermons of Peter, according to Papias, that Mark gathered his incidents and anecdotes about Jesus that chiefly make up his gospel. Nor would such a pitiful and convincing story have been invented, though it seemed so perfectly to fulfill Jesus' gloomy estimate—"Before the cock crows twice, you will disown me three times!"—of the value of Peter's brave protestations. There was no effort to expatiate on the cowardice of the disciples; the fact is simply but eloquently stated, with neither apology nor reproof.

And yet Peter was the bravest of them; he was the only one, according to the original story in Mark, who was anywhere near, and his position was certainly one to shake the stoutest heart. The situation had got completely out of hand; Jesus was on his way to the governor's court, and anything might happen there. To join him now was practically certain death. Peter's ideas of following Jesus had not previously contemplated anything so disastrous. He and his companions had been looking at a far brighter picture, with themselves in the high places of a new order.

Jesus' gloom at the supper had seemed to them little more than a momentary weakness. But now events were putting a somber meaning into his strange words.

The coming of daylight made it possible for the councilors to hold something like a regular meeting; the Sanhedrin never met at night, for then the gates of the temple were shut. Various irregularities about the trial of Jesus before the Sanhedrin have been pointed out. It was not held in the temple, where it always met; there is no parallel for a meeting at the high priest's house. A sentence of conviction could not be passed on the same day as the trial; it must go over to the next day; but the early morning meeting did not cover this point, for by the Jewish reckoning what we call Thursday night was a part not of Thursday but of Friday. The whole proceeding shows great precipitancy on the part of the council.

As soon as it was daylight, Jesus was duly condemned and bound, and, escorted by the council, was taken to the Roman governor, Pilate. For under the Romans, the Jews had no authority to impose and execute a sentence of death, which is what they demanded. This is Pilate's first appearance in the original gospel narrative, as Mark and Matthew reveal it. He had been governor of Judea for three or four years, having succeeded Valerius Gratus in A.D. 26. His residence was probably the palace Herod had built for himself in Jerusalem, in the middle of the west side of the city, near the present Jaffa gate.

It must have rudely disturbed the governor's comfortable routine to be called upon so early in the morning by his

Jewish neighbors from the high priest's palace, a quarter of a mile away, but he was now used to such calls, as he had already been embroiled with the Jerusalem population. The charge they brought against Jesus was evidently that he called himself the Messiah, which to Pilate could only mean that he meant to launch a revolution to make himself king. To defend the Roman authority against such occasional national outbursts was the prime duty of the governor. He therefore simply asked Jesus,

"Are you the King of the Jews?"

Jesus evidently understood this as referring to his being the Messiah, for he answered,

"Yes!"

Strangely enough, Pilate did not seem to think this settled it. He was haunted by the suspicion that the Sanhedrin was jealous of Jesus, and was trying on that account to put an end to him. The high priests continued to accuse him, and Pilate again asked him,

"Have you no answer to make? See what charges they are making against you!"

But Jesus was silent. He made no further answers, and Pilate was surprised. The hearing was interrupted at this point by another matter being brought before the governor by the arrival of a delegation to ask the governor in honor of the Passover festival to free a prisoner for whom they petitioned. The man they had in mind was a revolutionary named Barabbas, who had been arrested with others in a recent murderous outbreak. So when the crowd of people presented itself to ask that he be the prisoner to be released,

Pilate seized the opportunity to suggest to them that they make Jesus their nominee, and asked them,

"Do you want me to set the king of the Jews free for you?" He was evidently convinced that Jesus was not likely to be a peril to public order in Judea. This would of course have defeated the plans of the high priests, and they instigated the newcomers to stick to their original purpose of getting him to set Barabbas free. When Pilate put it to a viva-voce vote, and asked them,

"Which of the two do you want me to release to you?" without hesitation they cried,

"Barabbas!"

Pilate pursued this play-acting at democratic action, probably hoping he could get them to vote for releasing Jesus too, and said,

"Then what shall I do with the man you call the king of the Jews?"

They shouted back, "Crucify him!"

Pilate was shocked himself at such ferocity, and tried to labor with them:

"Why, what has he done that is wrong?"

But they shouted all the louder, "Crucify him!"

Outwitted at his own game, Pilate could see no way to get around it. He wanted to satisfy the crowd, so he set Barabbas free, as they demanded, and after flogging Jesus, probably to weaken him so as to shorten his life, he handed him over to a squad of soldiers to be crucified. So casually and flippantly the thing was done.

CHAPTER XVIII

The Crucifixion and the Resurrection

Matthew, writing after the fall of Jerusalem, with all its horrors and carnage, which of course he believed to be the Jews' punishment for crucifying Jesus, relates that Pilate was so shocked at the upshot of his slipshod efforts to get somebody else to take the responsibility for letting Jesus go that he called for water and solemnly washed his hands before the crowd, saying,

"I am not responsible for this man's death; you must see to it yourselves!"

To which the crowd actually replied with the cry,

"His blood be on us and on our children!"—thus as it were accepting the responsibility and calling down God's vengeance upon the next generation.

And Luke reports that Pilate in his efforts to evade responsibility for settling the case of Jesus found in his examination that he was from Galilee, and sent him over to the house of Herod Antipas, who had come up to Jerusalem for the feast, but that Antipas, though glad to have his curiosity about seeing him satisfied, settled nothing, and soon sent him back. Antipas would have been quite willing to let things take their course about Jesus, whom his minions had already menaced in Galilee and in Trans-Jordan. He must have been relieved to see that Jesus was not John the Baptist, risen from the dead, as he had feared, but another man altogether.

But Mark's narrative proceeds with a stern restraint that is positively amazing. It is strangely objective; all the more poignant because no pity, no sympathy find expression in it. The soldiers took Jesus inside the courtyard of the Palace, and called the whole battalion together to see the man who was about to be executed. They dressed Jesus up in a red or purplish cloak, such as soldiers wore, made a wreath of thorns and crowned him with it, in mockery of his royalty, and shouted,

"Long live the king of the Jews!"

They struck him over the head with the stick, spat at him, and knelt down and pretended to do homage to him. Of course in a time when one emperor, Augustus, in his shows, had set ten thousand men to fighting each other to death to entertain the Roman public, life counted for very little. When the soldiers had finished making sport of him, they took off the purple cloak and put his own clothes back on him, and set out with him for the place of crucifixion.

This was probably north of the city, not far outside the wall, and they doubtless left the city by a gate near the present Damascus gate, though just what its name was is not certain. Jesus was weakened by the fearful flogging or scourging he had undergone, and it was not possible for him to keep up and carry the crossbeam of his cross to the place of execution, as the prisoner was expected to do. The soldiers accordingly seized upon a passer-by, coming into the city from the country, and forced him to turn around and go with them, carrying it on his back. The man was from Cyrene in North Africa, and his name was Simon. Mark says he was the father of Alexander and Rufus, who were apparently well known to his Roman readers.

The place to which they went for the crucifixion was called Golgotha, an Aramaic word meaning skull, either from its association with executions or from the configuration of the ground. It has never been positively identified. There they offered him the drugged wine mercifully provided by women of Jerusalem, to dull the senses of condemned criminals, but he would not drink it.

Even in our days of new and refined cruelties, crucifixion is so brutal and cruel as hardly to bear description. Jesus was stripped of his clothes; his hands were nailed to the crossbeam. It was then raised and fastened to the upright, which was not as tall as Christian art has represented it. A peg between his thighs partly supported his body. His feet were then fastened with nails to the upright, and he was left to die of exhaustion and hunger, which might last for days. The proceedings before Pilate had been so hurried that it was only nine o'clock when he was put on the cross. The squad of soldiers were entitled to his clothes, as their perquisites for their work, and after dividing them by lot they, with the centurion in charge, sat down to keep watch, and see that no one tried to release him. They also hung the customary placard or piece of board above his head, with his name and his crime chalked on it. It read,

"The king of the Jews."

Two robbers who were slated for execution were crucified at the same time, one at his right and one at his left, which increased if possible the degradation of his end. The place was near the highway, and people passing along on their ways to or from the city paused to jeer at the dying man. Mark describes them as acquainted with the charge against him, of meaning to tear down the temple and build one in three days.

"Come down from the cross," they shouted, "and save yourself!"

A delegation from the Sanhedrin was also in attendance, to see that their wishes were carried out. They exchanged satisfied comments upon the situation. A crucifixion was no such frightful novelty to them as it would be to us.

"He has saved others," they would say ironically, "but he can't save himself! Let this Christ, the king of Israel, come down from the cross now, so that we may see it and believe!"

Even the wretched men crucified with him found some relief in joining in his abuse.

We have seen that Peter is the most probable source for much if not all the material the Gospel of Mark preserves; he was the first apostle called, for he always outstripped his brother Andrew, and was evidently the spirited, expressive member of the pair; as we have seen, it was evidently he and he alone that even ventured to hang about the long night-session at the high priest's palace. Did he also follow the wretched band that moved at daylight to the governor's residence, and finally out of the city to the place of execution? Or was it only those devoted women that had followed Jesus from Galilee that heard and reported the taunts and cries of those dreadful hours? Some of them certainly looked on from a distance—Mary of Magdala, Mary the mother of James and Joseph, and the mother of James and John.

At noon darkness overspread the land, and lasted till three o'clock. At three o'clock Jesus gave a great cry. It was the first line of the twenty-second Psalm, in Aramaic,

"My God, my God, why have you forsaken me?"— words of the utmost despair, though the Psalm itself goes on to end with deliverance. The first words, *Eloi, Eloi,* sound to the bystanders like a cry to Elijah.

"See!" they said, "he is calling for Elijah!"

One of them ran and soaked a sponge in common wine, and put it on the end of a stick, and held it up to him to drink, saying,

"Let us see whether Elijah does come to take him down!"

But Jesus gave a loud cry and expired.

And it is part of the amazing candor of this terrific narrative of Mark that it should end with this bitter cry of disillusion, disappointment, and despair.

His last intelligible cry may have been in delirium. But the early church saw in it his fulfillment of a Messianic picture in the Psalm, where God delivers his beloved out of the deepest despair.

There were no women present at the Last Supper, but of all Jesus' following only women, it would seem, stood by him to the end. And women have bulked largely in the Christian following ever since. This is no commonplace; look at its great rivals in the field of religion, Judaism, Mohammedanism! What have they for women? They are men's religions, and frankly so. And for that last terrible scene, the six hours of agony and delirium on the cross, we have only the memories of the women who at a little distance waited and listened.

And this, we must remember, was no peaceful death-bed; it was just as far from it as possible. Crucifixion was a death of torture. It is a pity modern faddists have picked the word up and taken out of it all its meaning, speaking lightly of "crucifying" one another! And too much must not be made of what the women and the bystanders understood Jesus was muttering or screaming from the cross. Even the words just quoted were differently understood by those near by. And later echoes from his lips found a place in the Gospel of Luke.

It was at three that the great cry from the twenty-second Psalm burst from his lips. But apparently before that, as Luke records it, one of the two thieves abused him, but the other reproved him, and asked Jesus to remember him when he came into his kingdom. Jesus answered,

"I tell you, you will be in Paradise with me today!"

And finally at three o'clock, Jesus said,

"Father, I intrust my spirit to your hands!"

This is a far more tranquil end than Mark and Matthew record. Some manuscripts of Luke, though not the most ancient ones, preserve also the beautiful prayer for his enemies, uttered when they were about to crucify him,

"Father, forgive them, for they do not know what they are doing!" Certainly the words nobly express what must have been Jesus' attitude, from all we know of him.

When the captain in charge of the execution saw how he expired, he said, "This man was certainly a son of God!" Perhaps he was a follower of Stoic religion, like Epictetus, who believed the great legendary heroes of Greece, like Hercules, by their unselfishness and heroism achieved sonship to God.

To bury the unclaimed Jewish dead had long been a pious practice among the Jews. The Book of Tobit, two hundred years before Christ, tells how Tobit had done it at the risk of his life. There were still men of equal devotion in Jerusalem, and one of them, Joseph of Arimathaea, a highly respected member of the Jewish council, now made himself responsible for Jesus' burial. He applied to Pilate for his body. Pilate could hardly believe that he was already dead, and sent for the captain to ask him whether it was really so. When he found out that it was, he gave Joseph permission to take the body. Joseph was probably all the more anxious to receive it, because at sunset the Sabbath would begin, and to have a dead Jew hanging on a cross by the high road on the Sabbath would be very highly offensive to Jewish sensibilities. The Jews also had strong views, as we have seen, on the defilement produced by contact with the dead.

The Jews were accustomed to bury their dead immediately, on the day on which they died. It was in haste, therefore, and without the usual anointing that Jesus was taken down from the cross and carried off to burial. The Sabbath, moreover, was close at hand. But Joseph had a rock-cut tomb in the broken ground north of the city and not far from the place of the crucifixion. He bought a linen sheet, had Jesus taken down from the cross and wrapped in it, and then laid him in this tomb, which probably had room for two or more bodies, for it was entered by a doorway in the rock, before which a circular stone was rolled to serve as a door. The faithful Galilean women who had followed Jesus from Galilee, Mary of Magdala, and Mary, Joseph's mother, witnessed Joseph's action and followed Jesus' body to the tomb. They noted the spot, for they meant to come back after the Sabbath to bring spices and anoint his body.

For a little while the cruel death of Jesus must have seemed to those who loved and followed him the bitter, chilling end of all their hopes. It is one of the paradoxes of history, indeed the chief such paradox, that it was just the opposite. Our earliest account of the amazing sequel is from the hand of Paul, who twenty-five years later wrote to the Corinthians about it. He had told them of it years before, when he first visited Corinth in A.D. 50, for he regarded it as the most important thing he had to tell —how Jesus was raised from the dead and appeared, first

to Cephas (the Aramaic word for Peter) and then to the
twelve (I Corinthians 15:5). It was evidently Peter who
first became conscious of the presence of Christ with him.
Paul apparently thought of this experience as quite of the
same kind as his own, on the Damascus road, on the occasion of his conversion, for he goes on to include that in the
list of such experiences (verse 8). But especial interest
attaches to the appearance to the twelve, for the Gospel of
Mark evidently ended, and culminated, in an account of
it, just as Matthew does.

It is on the eve of the account of this that the Gospel of
Mark breaks off abruptly—16:8. I suppose that its complete absorption in the later and religiously superior Gospel
of Matthew led to its disuse and neglect until, when the
four gospels were collected and published, about A.D. 115-
120, only a defective copy of Mark could be found for the
purpose. We cannot be too thankful that the publishers
of the collection nevertheless included it with the other
three. Two different conclusions have been added to it
after verse 8, in later manuscripts, but they are evidently
of no great antiquity or authority, for they say nothing
about the reunion in Galilee which had just been mentioned in Mark 16:7. This was not a new idea; as they
were leaving the upstairs room after the Passover supper,
Jesus had told them, Mark 14:28, "After I am raised to life
again I will go back to Galilee before you," and the apostles
had definitely in mind the mountain in Galilee that he
meant.

For the lost ending of Mark is unmistakably preserved

for us in the closing paragraphs of the Gospel of Matthew. Matthew, we can see, is faithfully copying everything of significance in Mark; he has done so from the very first, so that we can actually find fifteen-sixteenths of all Mark says reproduced in Matthew. Should this be thought an exaggeration, we may remember that Canon Streeter said he found nineteen-twentieths of Mark in Matthew! But in these closing pages particularly, while Matthew has much to add, he is meticulously incorporating into his narrative all that Mark affords. From Matthew 27:1 on, except for four or five scattered verses, hardly a clause or even a phrase of Mark's account is left out by Matthew. And where our Mark breaks off, Matthew goes right on with the story Mark has been leading up to—the reunion with Jesus at their rendezvous in Galilee. This has been specifically anticipated twice in the Gospel of Mark. Matthew tells how the eleven disciples went to Galilee, to the mountain to which Jesus had directed them. There they saw him and bowed down before him, though some were in doubt about it—a candid observation which in itself shows it was not a physical appearance. This is the appearance to the twelve mentioned by Paul in I Corinthians.

Then he gave them their great commission. He had confined his own work to his own people, the Jews. But the time has come to undertake the great mission, to the heathen world. They are to go and make disciples of all the heathen, and to teach them to observe all that he has commanded. And he will be with them always, to the very close of the age.

That he is to be with them always, to the very end, shows that it is not as a physical presence that he has come back to them, but as a spiritual one. As Dr. Buttrick once put it, "Their memory of him quickened to a presence!" The thing we most crave about our beloved departed is not so much their physical reanimation, but rather just this sense of their living presence with us, in our hearts, in guidance, sympathy, companionship and counsel. A physical presence if real could be in only one place at a time, but what the early church felt was Jesus' presence with every Christian heart, all over the ancient world.

And this became and remained the fundamental conviction of the early church. It was the experience of Paul, and the key to the Gospel of John. Paul became the great developer of this thought, though it was the Gospel of John that implemented it supremely. Christ by his death opens a new life to the believer; we have died with Christ, and risen with him to a new life (Romans 6). "The gift God gives is eternal life through union with Christ Jesus our Lord." God's spirit has really taken possession of us (Romans 8). Unless men have Christ's spirit, they do not belong to Christ. But if Christ is in their hearts their spirits will have life. This union with Christ makes them all sons of God through their faith (Galatians 3:26). In fact this idea is on almost every page of Paul's letters. Christ is in them. Living means Christ. Christ is everything, and in us all. He is our true life. In union with him, we are all one. It is no longer Paul that lives, but Christ that lives in him.

Paul, who had never seen him or heard him, in his bodily presence, caught from him his great sense that religion was not a legislation, and could not be reduced to one, and also caught his great vision of the love of God and love for men, of which John afterward made so much in John 3:16 and I John 4:8, 9. These passages owe much to Romans 5:5-8 and I Corinthians 13.

For the Gospel of John begins where Paul left off. It declares that Jesus has come back to trusting hearts as the Holy Spirit, the Comforter, the Helper, the Counselor, which would guide them into the full truth. The more Pharisaic idea, that Jesus' resurrection was a physical reanimation, played a very brief role in the serious thinking of the ancient church. After forty days, Luke declares, he ascended into the sky, the place, as Luke supposed, of heaven. But it was John's thought of his return, as an inward spiritual presence, that guided and inspired the primitive church and armed it with a spiritual force that was indomitable. It was another John, the Christian prophet of Ephesus, who felt that presence in his prison on the Island of Patmos. It was no arm of flesh on which the great figures of the later church leaned for support. Their most precious conviction was that they were actually "in Christ," in union with Christ, united to him, in communion and communication with him. It was this that purified their hearts and made them equal to any challenge or demand. Jesus had opened their way to God and they believed was still their great companion.

It was from this point of view that the Gospel of John

was written, reflecting the Christians' experience of Christ. They now knew him to be the bread of life, the water of life, the light of the world, who gave sight to the blind, healed the sick, and raised the spiritually dead. So much of John is clearly figurative and allegorical, although the parable, Jesus' characteristic form of teaching, is altogether absent. He lighted the way to knowledge, truth and freedom, great words in the old Greek world and great words today. A special blessing is pronounced upon those who have not seen him but have believed (20:29), and the great religious experience open to such, and a future life with him, are wonderfully set forth in the upper-room discourse. Through his spiritual presence believers are to be united with him as branches are united to a vine. The coming of Christ to the world and his work in it are shown to be, as Paul had felt (Romans 5:5-8), the supreme manifestation of the love of God.

He had already proved to be, in Christian experience, the way to God, and veritable truth and life, as he was to prove for subsequent centuries, and still proves to be today.

Names and Subjects

231

Quotations and References

241

PALESTINE
Sidon
Zarephath
Tyre
SYRIA
Damascus
ABILENE
PHOENICIA
Caesarea Philippi
ITUREA
Merom
TETRARCHY OF PHILIP
Gischala
GALILEE
Chorazin
Bethsaida
Capernaum
Chersa
Magdala
Sea of Galilee
Tiberias
Nazareth
Nain
Gadara
DECAPOLIS
MEDITERRANEAN SEA
Ptolemais
Carmel
Caesarea